About This Book

Why is this topic important?

Sound bites. Tag lines. Slogans. One-liners. The thirty-second spot. The sixty-second take. Small chunks of information dished up in short snippets of time. In television-dominated cultures, learners are used to this mode of information delivery: short and quick. Lengthy lectures are out. Short information chunks are in. Keeping this trend in mind, and using what we know about learning that sticks, those of us who are involved in the business of educating others need to design and deliver classes and programs that use shorter segments of time more effectively. We need to create learning experiences that are built on two fundamental learning principles of the twenty-first century: *shorter segments of instruction are better than longer ones, and learners remember more when they are involved in the learning.* Educating others becomes more effective, and less costly, when trainers use their time—and their learner's time—more efficiently. Involving learners before, during, and after short segments of instruction is also the basis of brain-compatible training, that is, teaching in ways that the human brain learns best.

What can you achieve with this book?

The Ten-Minute Trainer helps you make the most of your training time. This practical, grab-it-and-go book gives you 150 ways to use teachable moments—snippets of time in which you can reinforce the learning in powerful and memorable ways. This resource also gives you a simple and practical blueprint, based on how the human brain naturally learns, for designing and delivering training quickly and effectively. You will discover the brain research that supports short, quick instructional methods, and new ways to motivate learners and increase their ability to remember and use what they learn. With *The Ten-Minute Trainer* as your guide, you will involve training participants in their own learning without sacrificing any training content. Best of all, you will be an expert at teaching a lot in a little time.

How is this book organized?

Because your reading time is precious, this book gives you the "how to" information first.

Part One contains 150 ways to use short segments of time to help learners review, remember, and apply important information. From the collection of "Got a Minute?" activities to the "Take Five!" games, these hands-on strategies increase learner motivation, interest, and involvement. They also help move learning into long-term memory. All the activities are from sixty seconds to ten minutes in length.

Part Two gives you the practical brain research upon which this book is based. It also explains two powerful instructional tools—the Learning Compass and the Training Map—to help you design and deliver training in less time and with better long-term results. Finally, Part Two shows you how to include the book's concepts and activities in your own training by using five Power-Hour Training Templates.

Part Three offers you four "Get a CLUE!" elements to increase learner motivation and retention, "What's a Picture Worth?" suggestions for making your training more image-rich, ways to check for understanding, and a unique training activity called "Station Rotation."

You'll also find a collection of Remarkable Resources to complement *The Ten-Minute Trainer.*

About Pfeiffer

Pfeiffer serves the professional development and hands-on resource needs of training and human resource practitioners and gives them products to do their jobs better. We deliver proven ideas and solutions from experts in HR development and HR management, and we offer effective and customizable tools to improve workplace performance. From novice to seasoned professional, Pfeiffer is the source you can trust to make yourself and your organization more successful.

Essential Knowledge Pfeiffer produces insightful, practical, and comprehensive materials on topics that matter the most to training and HR professionals. Our Essential Knowledge resources translate the expertise of seasoned professionals into practical, how-to guidance on critical workplace issues and problems. These resources are supported by case studies, worksheets, and job aids and are frequently supplemented with CD-ROMs, Web sites, and other means of making the content easier to read, understand, and use.

Essential Tools Pfeiffer's Essential Tools resources save time and expense by offering proven, ready-to-use materials—including exercises, activities, games, instruments, and assessments—for use during a training or team-learning event. These resources are frequently offered in looseleaf or CD-ROM format to facilitate copying and customization of the material.

Pfeiffer also recognizes the remarkable power of new technologies in expanding the reach and effectiveness of training. While e-hype has often created whizbang solutions in search of a problem, we are dedicated to bringing convenience and enhancements to proven training solutions. All our e-tools comply with rigorous functionality standards. The most appropriate technology wrapped around essential content yields the perfect solution for today's on-the-go trainers and human resource professionals.

Pfeiffer
www.pfeiffer.com

Essential resources for training and HR professionals

The Ten-Minute Trainer

150

Ways to Teach It Quick and Make It Stick!

Sharon L. Bowman
Foreword by Dave Meier

Pfeiffer
A Wiley Imprint
www.pfeiffer.com

Acquiring Editor: Martin Delahoussaye

Director of Development: Kathleen Dolan Davies

Production Editor: Nina Kreiden

Editor: Suzanne Copenhagen

Manufacturing Supervisor: Becky Carreño

Illustrations: Mary Gillot

Printing 10 9 8 7

To Mom:

"You played a well game, girl,"
and you would have been so proud
of this "real" book.

And to all the eager readers
who grab a handful of sixty-second ideas
and create unforgettable learning experiences
from quick snippets of time.

Contents

Foreword

What the Trainer's Trainer Says About
The Ten-Minute Trainer

In this bright and zesty book, Sharon Bowman reminds us again of the basic fact of all learning: it is only what the *learner* creates that is learned.

Boy, do we ever need to hear this—repeatedly. We in the training field often get hung up by the belief that it is the *instructor's* presentation that determines the quality of learning. And so we continue to rely on things such as the interminable PowerPoint® lecture as the centerpiece of our training programs.

But PowerPoint, overused, is nothing more than electronic chloroform. It knocks people out. Instead, our job as training professionals is to wake people up. Yes, *wake people up*—to their full potential for learning, for job success, and for a life that embraces the full mind, body, and spirit.

The Ten-Minute Trainer will certainly wake people up. It contains a gold mine of easy-to-use ideas for getting learners to talk, to think, to move, to create, to act—and thus to learn. And it contains a rapid design method for weaving these ideas together into effective learning programs.

Use this book as a resource. Refer to it often. Consult it when you're stuck. It will re-awaken you to what good learning really is—*a supreme act of creation on the part of the learner.*

The Ten-Minute Trainer is bound to make your job easier and more fun, and make you much more effective as a designer and facilitator of learning.

Count on it.

Dave Meier
Author of *The Accelerated Learning Handbook*
Director of the Center for Accelerated Learning
Lake Geneva, Wisconsin

Opening and Connections

What's in It for You?

Introducing You to *The Ten-Minute Trainer*

Quick Start

Mark-Up. Circle the answer to each question.

1. How long is the average length of a television drama, comedy, news, or documentary segment before a commercial break occurs?

   A. About 20 minutes.

   B. About 5 to 9 minutes.

   C. About 8 to 12 minutes.

   D. Not long enough.

2. How long are the commercial breaks between show segments?

   A. They feel like forever.

   B. Probably around 15 minutes.

   C. Closer to 8 minutes

   D. About 4 to 6 minutes.

Answers: If you circled 1C and 2D, congratulations. You probably watch a lot of television—or you are really good at estimating time. Either way, in this chapter you'll discover the connection between television and training, and why this connection is important to you.

It used to be that most face-to-face instruction was pretty much straight lecture, with learners listening (maybe taking some notes) and the subject matter expert doing all the talking.

Here's the truth about that type of teaching: it never really worked well to begin with and it still doesn't work well. Especially now, it needs to change because learners, as well as entire cultures, have changed how they take in information.

On the up side, most of us who have the job of educating others, and who are good at what we do, have already moved from lecture-based methods of instruction to more learner-friendly methods. We try to involve our learners in a variety of ways to increase interest, motivation, learning, and retention.

On the down side, it takes time—and lots of it—to continuously think of new ways to keep training participants motivated, interested, and involved. While we struggle with this dilemma, our learners have totally different learning expectations than folks did fifty years ago. And the biggest change in how people learn today, according to many researchers, stems from—you guessed it—television.

How TV Changed You and Me

"What has television got to do with face-to-face instruction?" you ask. The answer is simple. Television has

- *Conditioned* us to expect fast-paced, attention-getting methods of information delivery.

- *Reduced* the length of time that we pay attention by delivering information and entertainment in shorter and shorter segments of time.

- *Reawakened* us to the power of the image to teach, entertain, convince, and make a message memorable.

These changes aren't bad or good; they just are. As trainers, we can rail against them, rally for them, or simply understand and use them to create learning experiences that work better for our learners.

The changes in how people take in information have occurred in the world's cultures that are television-saturated, that is, where the majority of people watch two hours or more of programming every day. In the United States, that number is now approaching four hours.

Why Ten Minutes?

When we pay attention to what goes on in those two to four hours of television viewing, an interesting pattern of timing emerges. According to the American Association of Advertising Agencies and the Association of National Advertisers, Americans watch about forty minutes of programming and twenty minutes of commercials an hour. This means that in a fifteen-minute viewing segment, we see about ten minutes of an actual program and about five minutes of commercials. Variations to these numbers depend upon the broadcasting station itself, the changing federal and state regulations, the time of the day or evening, and the type of program. These numbers also differ depending upon the country and culture. Around the world, each country has its own regulatory laws concerning commercial break times, but the overall pattern is the same everywhere: *most television-dominated cultures are moving toward shorter program times and longer commercial break times.*

Those of us who help others learn need to take these changes into account when designing and delivering training. If we don't, we will lose many learners along the way, or learners will need remediation later because they will have forgotten most of what they heard. This does not mean that we need to dumb down our training. It does mean that we need to change our methods of instruction to meet the television-conditioned learning needs and shorter attention spans of our audiences. More specifically, it means that we should break up our information delivery into shorter lecture segments while increasing learner involvement throughout the training.

> **T**ake a **B**reak **Time It.** You don't have to take the advertising association's word for it. Run a quick test yourself. The next time you sit down to watch a major broadcasting station's prime-time programs, have a stopwatch handy. Time the program segments over a one-hour period. Also time the commercial breaks over that same period. Get an average of each. Jot down your numbers here:
>
> _____

The Brain Gain

One worthwhile outcome of television viewing is that it demonstrates the power and potential of an image-rich medium of learning. In that respect, it is very compatible with how the human brain really learns. The brain can absorb visual information at a much faster rate than verbal information. Television does just that: it delivers images in rapid-fire sequences, sending a lot of information to the brain in the medium the brain processes best—images. In contrast, traditional instruction, with its emphasis on lecture and listening, is a brain drain—numbing the neurons and damaging the dendrites with boredom, tediousness, and deadly dull learning.

In addition to being an image-rich medium, television is also brain-compatible in that it keeps the mind engaged by using a variety of constantly changing sounds and images. This sensory stimulation activates the part of the brain that responds to changing stimuli in order to stay awake and alert.

The connection between how television delivers its messages and how we, as trainers, deliver ours is clear. In order to create brain-compatible learning experiences, we need to include more imagery and change in our training. We must supplement our words with pictures, photos, cartoons, drawings, doodles, metaphors, analogies, stories, symbols, icons, and so forth. We should include three-dimensional imagery as well, such as physical movement, spatial activities, improvisation, and games that get the learner's whole body involved in the learning. We need to change more things during training: instructional strategies, presentation methods, room environment, learner involvement, and sensory stimuli. In other words, we must design and deliver training in ways that television viewers expect and that the human brain loves: *with short informational segments followed by quick breaks, and all of it packaged in high-energy, fast-paced, image-rich ways.*

Who Needs to Know?

If you give information to other people and you want them to learn it, remember it, and use it in some fashion, *The Ten-Minute Trainer* is written for you. It doesn't matter what you call yourself—teacher, trainer, instructor, educator, facilitator, human resource specialist, performance improvement technologist—it's the work you do that counts. *And your work is educating others so that they can become better at what they do or so that their lives improve because of what they learned.* Whether you are new to teaching and training or an experienced pro, your work is important, and this timely resource will help you do it even more successfully.

New Trainers. Read Part One first. Choose one or two activities to include in your scripted training. Simply slip them in where a natural break in information-delivery seems to occur. When you become comfortable with these activities, choose one or two more. Observe which ones work best for you, your learners, and the topics you teach. Keep these as part of your standard training delivery. Later, when you want more information about brain research and training design, read Part Two.

Experienced Trainers. Read Part Two first. Familiarize yourself with the brain research about effective learning and teaching. Use this information, and the activities in Part One, to fine-tune what you already do well. Substitute new activities for ones you always use but that don't excite you anymore. Experiment with the two design tools—the Learning Compass and the Training Map—and combine them with what you already know about effective training design.

Busy Trainers. Read this resource like a newspaper. Skim the Contents for chapter titles that interest you. Read those chapters first. Or use the book as a back-pocket resource when you want a quick activity and have only a short time to find one. Skip to what you need or want. Save the rest for later.

Twelve Benefits You'll Get from This Book

The Ten-Minute Trainer is based on two fundamental training principles of the twenty-first century: *shorter segments of instruction are better than longer ones, and learners remember more when they are involved in the learning.*
With these concepts in mind and this book as your guide, you will be able to

1. *Choose from 140 "Got a Minute?" activities* to include in your lectures so that your learners review, repeat, and remember important information (Part One).

2. *Use ten short "Take Five!" games* to RAP up the learning—reinforce, apply, and practice—so that learning is moved into long-term memory (Part One).

3. *Soak up ordinarily wasted instructional minutes* with thirty Time Sponges such as Quick Starts, Take a Break, and Early to Finish activities (Part One).

4. *Experiment with quick, high-energy ways* to involve your learners without sacrificing content (Part One).

5. *Apply two powerful instructional tools*—the Learning Compass and the Training Map—to shorten your training design and delivery time (Part Two).

6. *Use five Power-Hour Training Templates,* with any topic, any size group, and any age learner (Part Two).

7. *Organize your lecture time* so that your learners get the most from your instruction (Part Two).

8. *Understand the brain research* behind the concepts in *The Ten-Minute Trainer* (Part Two).

9. *Include four "Get a CLUE!" elements* to increase motivation and memory (Part Three).

10. *Make your training more image-rich*—by using graphics, cartoons, doodles, and more (Part Three).

11. *Change your concept of training time* as you use small but mighty seconds and minutes in creative, interesting, and memorable ways (Parts One, Two, and Three).

12. *Become a more time-efficient training professional* and be able to explain the what, why, and how of it all to your training colleagues (Parts One, Two, and Three).

Take a Break **Mark-Up.** Skim the list of benefits you'll get from this book and circle the three that, for you, are the most important. Use this list as a pre-assessment of what you want to get out of the book. Now label those three A, B, C in order of importance. If you're short on time, skip ahead to the parts of the book that contain that information and read them first.

It's Organized to Save You Time

Most busy trainers seldom have enough time to sit down and read a training book cover to cover. Often, they will flip quickly through books to find one or two activities that are easy to combine with what they already have planned to do. If this describes you, turn to Part One, which gives you the "how to" information first. Later, when you have more reading time, you can turn to Part Two, where you'll find the practical research upon which the book is based. In Part Three you'll find a number of other useful tools to increase learners' motivation and memory.

Part One Contains . . .
- "Got a Minute?" Activities to Help Learners Review, Repeat, and Remember. Each of these 140 activities lasts about sixty seconds and involves learners in a variety of hands-on, upbeat, thought-provoking ways. All you have to do is to

sprinkle your training with a few of these activities, including them where they seem to fit best or where you want a quick review before moving on to new information.

- "Take Five!" Games That Help Learners RAP It Up: Reinforce, Apply, and Practice. The ten games and activities are from five to ten minutes in length. Some are collaborative and some are competitive. You can use them with most topics and most audiences. Include them as openings, as closings, or when you want a longer review break between informational pieces.

Part Two Includes . . .

- "Attention Maker, Attention Breaker": The Recticular Activating System and Learning. You'll discover what attracts the attention of the human brain, for how long, and what you as a trainer can do to increase motivation, interest, and retention.

- "Three Brains in One": The Triune Brain and Learning. You'll find out why connections are so crucial to a successful learning experience, and how to create a safe learning community whatever the training topic or duration.

- "Let the Compass Be Your Guide": The Learning Compass and Learning the Natural Way. This instructional tool shows you how humans naturally learn and gives you four learning phases to guide you, as represented by the compass points.

- "Mapping Your Message": Making It Stick with the Training Map. Together with the Learning Compass, this training tool forms the easy-to-use blueprint that will enable you to design and deliver training in less time and with better long-term results.

- "Power-Hour Training Templates": Time-Saving Design and Delivery Tools. These five templates are easy-to-use instructional design tools that will save you time by combining your content with the ideas and activities from this book. The templates are excellent examples of how to use the Learning Compass and the Training Map. They also show you how to include the "Got a Minute?" and "Take Five!" training activities.

Part Three Contains . . .

- "Get a CLUE!" Four Elements to Increase Motivation and Memory in Learning. When you include all four elements in your training, you increase long-term retention while keeping learners interested, motivated, awake, and enthusiastic.

- "You Said It But Did They Get It?" How to Check for Understanding. Here are five ways to make sure learners understand, and can use, what they hear.
- "What's a Picture Worth?" The Importance of Imagery in Learning. You'll understand the human brain's need for images and how to include a variety of image-rich instructional strategies in your training.
- "Station Rotation": Learning a Lot in a Little Time. The Station Rotation activity is a powerful training strategy that has participants learning new concepts, reviewing learned concepts, practicing skills, applying what they've learned, and doing it all at the same time!

Walking the Talk

Inasmuch as a book can, this resource will model what it teaches: *short and quick is better than long and slow, and involving the learner (in this case, that's you, the reader) increases long-term retention of information.*

You'll be encouraged to participate along the way with three kinds of reader-centered activities. These are examples of the sixty-second activities in Part One and generally fall into the category of Time Sponges, that is, activities that connect you to the concepts while soaking up a minute or two of time. You have already done a few of these:

- Quick Start. This is an opening activity that will focus on what you already know or what you're about to learn regarding the concepts in the chapter.
- Take a Break. This is a review activity that will enhance your understanding of what you are learning.
- Early to Finish. This is a closing activity that will add to what you just learned or suggest ways to review the information in order to move it into long-term memory.

The book's format is informal, conversational, and easy and quick to read and use. But don't be fooled by its simplicity. The concepts are based on solid research (see the Remarkable Resources at the back of the book) and are presented in this easy-to-learn format in order to save you time.

The best thing about *The Ten-Minute Trainer* is that it will empower you, motivate you, and increase your energy level and enthusiasm for learning and training. It will get your creative juices flowing. It will spark lots of spin-off ideas—variations on activities that you'll come up with and that will work even better for you and your training participants. So relax, enjoy, experiment, and have fun with it all.

Wrapping It Up

With *The Ten-Minute Trainer,* you will polish what you already do well by using shorter segments of instruction followed by quick, learner-centered review activities. You will consistently turn passive listeners into active learners. You will design and deliver training that is both timely and terrific. You will tie everything you do to these two fundamental training principles: *shorter segments of instruction are better than longer ones, and learners remember more when they are involved in the learning.* To that end, welcome to a "teach it quick and make it stick" learning experience!

Take what you can use and let the rest go by.

—Ken Kesey

Early to Finish

Think and Write. To become more aware of how you use your training time, jot down your responses to these questions, then read the author's italicized comments.

- Who does most of the talking in a one-hour training segment, you or your learners?

_____

The person doing the most talking about the topic is doing the most learning. So, if that person is you, you are doing the most learning. According to most research, learners don't remember much after about twenty minutes or so of simply listening. But long-term memory increases measurably when learners say or do something every ten minutes with information presented to them. If you aren't sure how long you talk, have someone time your lectures.

- Where do you include most of the learning activities in a training hour (beginning, middle, end, or throughout)?

_____

In order for learners to remember more of what you teach them, you should space activities throughout the training. Shorter, more frequent activities are better than fewer, longer ones. The more you involve your learners in the learning, the more they will remember. Involvement can be done in simple, quick ways. If you aren't used to involving learners, begin by choosing one or two of the sixty-second activities in this book. Get comfortable with them and then experiment with a few more.

- What instructional strategies do you usually use during one hour of training? (Examples: lecturing, using visuals to enhance information, demonstrating a skill, including short quizzes, telling stories, asking questions, showing a video, facilitating a game.)

Whenever you change your instructional strategies, you engage the part of your learner's brain that thrives on changing stimuli. These changes help learners stay awake and alert throughout the training. Even during a one-hour training segment, using a variety of instructional strategies enhances learners' motivation and memory.

- How often do you use images in an hour training—and what kind do you use? (Examples: photos, cartoons, clip art, doodles, shapes, lines, stories, metaphors, analogies.)

Anytime you include an image—a cartoon with a computer slide, a metaphor to explain a procedure, a story to dramatize an important point, a physical movement along with a verbal fact—you increase the length of time learners will remember the information. If you aren't using images, begin with a few simple graphics to enhance your slides, charts, transparencies, and written or computerized materials. Or tell a story to illustrate a point you're making.

Part One

When They Do It, They Get It!

150 Activities to Make the Learning Stick

> ### Quick Start
>
> **Mark-Up.** All the activity names in Part One are listed below.
> Circle any that sound interesting to you or that you think you might
> be familiar with. As you read the chapters in Part One, you may discover that these
> activities are similar to ones you use or ones that you know by other names.
>
> | | | |
> |---|---|---|
> | Time Sponges | Quick Starts | Take a Break |
> | Early to Finish | Connections | Pair Shares |
> | Shout Outs | Mark-Ups | Signals |
> | Doodles | Think and Write | Pop-Ups |
> | Tickets Out | Action Plans | Celebrations |
> | Gallery Walk | Take a Stand | Grab That Spoon |
> | Place Your Order | Metaphor Magic | Let's Trade |
> | The Walkabout | Each One Teach One | Blackout Bingo |
> | Postcard Partners | | |

Sometimes in your work as a training professional you have probably felt as though your job is at "warp speed," with each training looming on the heels of the one before. You seem to stay one step ahead of where you have to be. You find yourself squeezing in moments (instead of hours) of study time in order to become even better at what you do. You often skim training books, looking for the activities you can put to use immediately and promising to read the rest of the material when you have the time.

   With that thought in mind, you'll find the practical, how-to activities listed in Part One up front, where you can get to them quickly. Later, when you have more time, you can read Part Two, which covers the brain research and training design tools that support using these short, quick activities in your training.

A Bird's-Eye View of 150 Activities

Here is what you'll find in Part One:

- An introduction to the "Got a Minute?" activities. This will explain the rationale for these sixty-second activities, what you can accomplish by using them, and some tips to keep in mind as you experiment with them.
- 140 "Got a Minute?" activities to help learners review, repeat, and remember important information.
- An introduction to the "Take Five!" games. This will explain why these five- and ten-minute activities are important, what you can accomplish by using them, and some tips to keep in mind.
- Ten "Take Five!" games to help learners RAP up the learning: reinforce, apply, and practice.

   Here is a more detailed list of the sixty-second activities and how you might use them in your training:

- *Connections.* These are opening activities that connect learners to each other, to what they already know about the training topic, and to what they want to learn.
- *Time Sponges.* Use these to soak up time at the opening, during a break, or when participants finish an activity or game early. Use them also as connection activities to connect learners to each other and to the training topic or concepts.
- *Pair Shares.* Use these as quick review exercises throughout the training.
- *Shout Outs.* Use these as opening activities to find out what learners already know about the topic. Use them also as quick review exercises.
- *Think and Write.* These are introspective review activities you can use throughout a training.
- *Signals.* Use these to check for understanding or as yes or no answers to verbal questions.

- *Doodles.* These are visual, right-brain ways of representing important facts or concepts.
- *Pop-Ups.* These are kinesthetic review exercises, that is, they include movement in the review process.
- *Mark-Ups.* With these, participants interact with written material by marking the text in various ways.
- *Tickets Out.* Use these as closing activities to help participants think about and evaluate what they learned.
- *Action Plans.* These are closing activities that encourage participants to make a commitment to use what they learned.
- *Celebrations.* These are closing activities that celebrate the learning with a high-energy, enthusiastic end to the training.

And here is a more detailed list of the five- and ten-minute games, along with how you might use them in your training:

- *Postcard Partners.* Use this as an opening activity to connect learners to each other and to the training topic or concepts.
- *The Gallery Walk.* This can be an opening activity, a review activity, or a closing exercise. Or use it as an ongoing activity throughout the training or during training breaks.
- *Take a Stand.* This is either an opening activity or a review activity when you want participants to discuss topic-related issues.
- *Grab That Spoon.* As a closing exercise, this is a competitive game for a general review. Or include each game round, that is, one question and answer, at various times throughout the training to review specific concepts.
- *Place Your Order.* Use this to review procedural concepts during the training, that is, information that needs to be learned in a certain order.
- *Metaphor Magic.* This is a creative, right-brain way of reviewing concepts, which makes learners think about what they have learned in unique and unusual ways. It can also be a creative closing activity.
- *Let's Trade.* Use this as a closing activity in which participants make a commitment to use what they have learned.
- *Each One Teach One.* Use this as a kinesthetic exercise to help learners practice skills or review information in an active, hands-on way.

- *The Walkabout.* This is a closing kinesthetic activity that is also high-energy and celebratory.
- *Blackout Bingo.* Use this as another high-energy, closing activity. It is also a kinesthetic review exercise.

Chunk It

In order to use these 150 activities in ways that will make them work best for your learners, you will need to "chunk" your material, that is, divide your information into shorter lecture segments. If you've never done this before, then the easiest way to begin is to cut your material in half. You will deliver both halves, but you will also include a sixty-second activity in between each half.

For example, if you're used to lecturing for an hour, lecture for thirty minutes instead. Then stop talking and lead the participants in a sixty-second review activity. After that, continue with the next thirty minutes of lecture. You can also include a sixty-second activity at the beginning of the first thirty minutes and at the end of the last thirty minutes.

If your normal lecture time is about a half hour, take two thirty-minute lecture pieces and divide that material into four fifteen-minute segments. Include sixty-second activities at the beginning, the end, and in between each of the four segments for a total of five short, quick activities in an hour.

Your goal in chunking your material is to get close to the ten-minute mark, not only because of the television-affected, shortened attention spans of your participants, but also because the human brain learns better that way (see Part Two for the brain research that supports the ten-minute lecture).

Remember, ten minutes of information delivery is the goal, not the rule. You decide what's appropriate for you, for the material you're teaching, and for the learners who attend your training. Sometimes your lectures will take a little longer, sometimes they will be a little shorter.

Not sure about how long you lecture? Use a timer while rehearsing portions of your material. Or have a friend time you as you talk. Be aware that time seems to fly when you're the one standing in front of an audience. But for those who have to remain seated for long periods without doing anything except listening, time often seems to crawl.

Wrapping It Up

So what's the bottom line? Simply this: these 150 activities aren't about you. They are about your learners—including them, involving them, honoring them and what they already know, and making sure they remember the concepts you're teaching them. When you use these activities in your training, the underlying message you give learners is a powerful one: *they are important, they matter, and the real learning comes from them.*

As with any skill, the more you practice it, the better you are at doing it. The more you use these activities—varying them and experimenting with them—the better results you'll get in terms of learners' increased interest, involvement, and long-term retention of important information.

Go ahead—jump in. The water's fine. Choose an activity or two from this part of the book, include them in your next training, and watch what happens. And by the way, in addition to learning more and remembering it longer, your learners will think you walk on water!

Most people tire of a lecture in ten minutes.
Clever people do it in five.
Sensible people never go to lectures at all.

—Stephen Loncock

———— ♟ ————

Early to Finish

Action Plan. Go back to the Quick Start at the beginning of this chapter. Choose two of the items you circled and write them in the space below. Then flip to those activities and read them first. Plan to use them in your next training.

Got a Minute?

Sixty-Second Activities to Help Learners Repeat, Review, and Remember

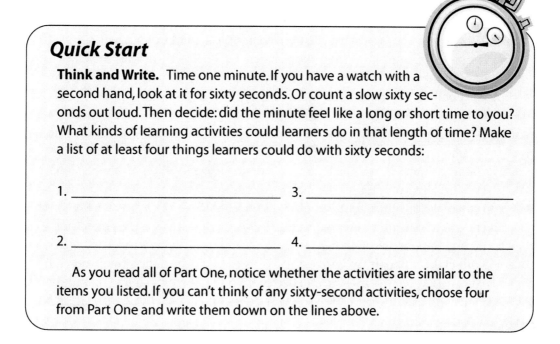

Quick Start

Think and Write. Time one minute. If you have a watch with a second hand, look at it for sixty seconds. Or count a slow sixty seconds out loud. Then decide: did the minute feel like a long or short time to you? What kinds of learning activities could learners do in that length of time? Make a list of at least four things learners could do with sixty seconds:

1. _____   3. _____

2. _____   4. _____

As you read all of Part One, notice whether the activities are similar to the items you listed. If you can't think of any sixty-second activities, choose four from Part One and write them down on the lines above.

Picture This

You are feeling a great deal of work-related stress so you decide to take a one-hour stress management workshop offered at your local community college. You walk into the classroom and immediately notice the large screen in front of the room on which is printed:

Quick Start.

After reading this, introduce yourself to three people seated near you.

Tell them what you want to learn in this workshop.

Be ready to state what they say when asked to do so.

This is your Expert Group.

You sit down and start chatting with two people seated to your left and right. After a couple of minutes, the workshop instructor begins by asking the class to state a number between one and ten. Someone speaks up, "Six." The instructor responds, "Let's list six things you want to learn in this session. You can shout out one of the things you heard your expert group say." People take turns stating what they discussed while the instructor counts the statements. Then she summarizes what people said and links the summary to the goals for the workshop. Finally, she introduces herself as Diana and gives a brief outline of the session.

As the workshop progresses, Diana stops after every ten minutes of lecture and tells you to do various things with what you've just heard. For example, one time she directs you to take one minute and think about what she has presented and then write one sentence explaining it in your own words on an index card. Another time she directs you to pair up with one of your expert group members and chat for sixty seconds about the most important fact you've learned so far. Yet another time she tells you to stand and stretch. Then she says, "In order to earn your chair back, tell your expert group one technique for lessening stress that hasn't yet been mentioned in this workshop. When everyone in your expert group has done this, you can all sit back down."

Toward the end of the hour, Diana tells you to write "I plan to . . ." on the back of your index card. She explains, "Write an action plan on your card. This is what you are making a commitment to do the next time you find yourself in a stressful, work-related situation. If you have time, read your action plan to your expert group." She gives you a minute to do this.

While you are sharing your action plan with your expert group, Diana passes out small toy whistles to everyone. She whistles to get the attention of the class and then summarizes the major points of the workshop. Then she says, "This whistle is a souvenir of this workshop. It will also remind you to whistle while you work, that is, find ways to lessen your own stress. Now whistle if you learned what you came to learn this evening." A resounding chorus of whistles follows. She says, "Whistle if you can use what you learned at work tomorrow." More whistles follow. She ends with, "Give your expert group a high-five and whistle to let them know how much you enjoyed learning with them this evening." Laughter erupts throughout the room as everyone whistles one more time while they all give each other high-fives.

You leave feeling energized by the workshop and certain that you can use the positive stress management ideas the next day. You realize what a unique workshop this was because everyone was involved in the learning the entire hour. What you might not realize is that Diana used a number of simple, sixty-second activities to keep you involved: a Quick Start, a Think and Write, a Pair Share, a Pop-Up, an Action Plan, and a Celebration. Whatever they were called, the teaching techniques must have worked because you're planning to manage your own stress differently as a result of what you learned.

Why Sixty Seconds?

Even though you have a large amount of material to cover in a short amount of time, you'll find it easy to sprinkle one-minute activities throughout your training. A sixty-second activity is doable when a sixty-minute activity is not. A sixty-second activity is short enough to hold your learners' attention, yet long enough to provide a quick review of a segment of information. And including one-minute activities keeps your training participants attentive, interested, involved, and learning.

What Sixty Seconds Can Do

One sixty-second activity may not seem like much. After all, it passes by so fast. But include a different sixty-second activity every ten to twenty minutes of your lecture time, and your learners will

- *Repeat* what they just heard, which will help them remember it longer.
- *Review* material in a number of creative ways.

- *Think* about what they just learned.
- *Keep* their minds alert and attentive.
- *Reenergize* their bodies.
- *Become* active participants in their own learning.
- *Link* what they just learned to what they already know.
- *Feel* that what they already know is worthwhile.
- *Increase* short-term memory.
- *Move* some of the information into long-term memory.
- *Build* a safe learning community, where they can talk, ask questions, laugh, and make mistakes.
- *Have* fun while they learn.
- *Buy* into what is being taught.
- *Lessen* any resistance to the learning experience that they may have.
- *Seek* out additional learning experiences that make them feel as good as this one.

Another Bird's-Eye View of the "Got a Minute?" Activities

So that you don't have to flip back to Chapter One, here again is the detailed list of the sixty-second activities:

- *Connections.* These are opening activities that connect learners to each other, to what they already know about the training topic, and to what they want to learn.
- *Time Sponges.* Use these to soak up time at the opening, during a break, or when participants finish an activity or game early. Use them also as connection activities to connect learners to each other and to the training topic or concepts.
- *Pair Shares.* Use these as quick review exercises throughout the training.
- *Shout Outs.* Use these as opening activities to find out what learners already know about the topic. Use them also as quick review exercises.
- *Think and Write.* These are introspective review activities to be used throughout a training.
- *Signals.* Use these to check for understanding or as yes or no answers to verbal questions.

- *Doodles.* These are visual, right-brain ways of representing important facts or concepts.
- *Pop-Ups.* These are kinesthetic review exercises, that is, they include movement in the review process.
- *Mark-Ups.* With these, participants interact with written material by marking the text in various ways.
- *Tickets Out.* Use these as closing activities to help participants think about and evaluate what they learned.
- *Action Plans.* These are closing activities that encourage participants to make a commitment to use what they learned.
- *Celebrations.* These are closing activities that celebrate the learning with a high-energy, enthusiastic end to the training.

¡Tips and Variations!

What You Say. For each of the 140 "Got a Minute?" activities, what you say is printed in italics. These are suggestions only. Please adapt them to your training style, topic, and audience.

Materials at Hand. For the activities that need certain materials, make sure that you have a sufficient number of items for everyone. So that you don't waste valuable training time, pass out the materials before the training, or have them ready and available on the tables or chairs when participants enter the room.

Explain the Why. If you feel it is necessary, preface the sixty-second activities with the *why* behind the *how.* Explain that these short snippets of review time will actually help participants remember more of the material when the training is over. In addition, you can post the "What Sixty Seconds Can Do" list in a visible place in the room and refer to it occasionally as a reminder of what the "take-aways" of activity are.

The Right to Pass. Let participants know that they have the right to pass on any activity, that is, they may simply observe if they so choose. This lessens any resistance that strong watchers (those who learn more by observing than by doing) may have. It also allows anyone who is tired of interacting to simply take a break from the activities while still remaining involved in the learning.

Have a Signal. Decide what the signal will be for getting the whole group's attention after the activity. You might simply raise your hand or sound a noisemaker. Model the signal so participants know what to expect.

Look Them Over. Skim the sixty-second activities in this section and choose a few that you would like to try, that fit your audience, or that appeal to your training style. Flag those pages and circle or highlight the activities so that you can find them quickly.

Use a Variety. Vary the sixty-second activities you use to keep learners interested and motivated. Take a look at the Power-Hour Training Templates in Part Two to see how you can use a different sixty-second activity every ten to twenty minutes.

Talk About It. If you have the time, or if you feel that it is important enough, follow the sixty-second activity with a brief processing minute during which you invite learners to tell the group what they learned from their participation.

The Teachable Moment. A sixty-second activity is a teachable moment—a snippet of time in which to reinforce learning in a powerful and memorable way. Sometimes these activities lead to other teachable moments, when learners get an unexpected insight about the material or about themselves that they wouldn't have gotten otherwise. Take time to explore these unplanned learning gems—they are value-added take-aways that learners will remember.

Keep It Short. Pay attention to your learners and stop the activity time before everyone finishes or before they get restless. With sixty seconds, that won't happen too often, but it's better to have learners wanting more rather than sitting there with nothing to do while waiting for you to continue. Err on the side of too short rather than too long.

Or Make It Longer. However, if participants are intensely involved in the activity, lengthen the time by another minute so that the learning doesn't abruptly stop.

Wrapping It Up

Sprinkling your lecture with sixty-second activities is a powerful way to make your teaching stick. You'll never look at a single training minute with the same mindset again. Instead, it will become a magical moment in which you turn passive listeners into active learners—over and over again.

An ounce of experience is worth a ton of theory.
—Benjamin Franklin

Early to Finish

Pair Share. Different trainers use sixty-second activities for different reasons. Look back over the "What Sixty Seconds Can Do" list and circle what you consider the three most important items. Ask another trainer or colleague to circle his or her three most important items. Then together, discuss any differences. What each of you considers important will, in turn, guide the choices you make with respect to the training activities you decide to use.

Connections

What Is a Connection?

A Connection is an opening activity that helps learners focus on what they know or want to know while also introducing themselves to the other learners. They do this by talking to other learners. A Connection differs from an icebreaker in that the latter is usually social and not topic-related, whereas the former always connects learners to the topic as well as to each other.

When you use a Connection as an opening activity, your learners do three important things. First, they connect to their own learning goals, that is, what they hope to get out of the training. Second, they connect to what they already know about the training topic so that they can link new learning to old. And third, they connect to the other learners (and, of course, to you) in order to form a learning community for the duration of the training.

What Does a Connection Do?

With a Connection activity, learners will

- *Form* a safe learning community with the other learners in the room.
- *Remind* themselves of their own personal learning goals.
- *Become* aware of what they already know about the training topic.
- *Focus* their energy on learning from the moment they enter the room.
- *Feel* a sense of belonging as well as safety.
- *Relax* into the learning experience.
- *Feel* a shift of energy in the room from the quiet, passive feeling that most people have when sitting with a group of strangers to a higher-energy, more open feeling experienced when sitting with new friends.
- *Recognize* that they are respected and honored by you and the other learners.
- *Get* a sense of positive expectation about the learning experience to come.

Getting Ready

Materials: For most of the Connection activities, no extra materials are necessary. For Connection #10, learners will need index cards and pens or pencils.

Setup: No special room setup is necessary.

Group Size: Any size group is fine.

Ten Connections

- **Connection #1:** *Quickly introduce yourself to someone seated near you and tell your new friend two things: what you want to learn today and one fact you already know about the training topic. Please make sure everyone around you has a partner. Triads are acceptable too.*

- **Connection #2:** *Introduce yourself to the person in front or behind you and ask your new friend to tell you three things he already knows about the training topic.*

- **Connection #3:** *The folks seated closest to you, or at your table, are your Expert Group for this training. Introduce yourself to them and tell them one thing you want to take away from this learning experience.*

- **Connection #4:** *Quickly shake hands with two people near you and tell them one question you want answered during this training.*

- **Connection #5:** *Stand and bow to three people standing close to you. Ask them who they are and why they are here today.*

- **Connection #6:** *Stand and form a small group with those around you. Share with your group what you want to learn today and what you already know about the topic.*

- **Connection #7:** *Stand and find one person in the room whom you don't yet know. Introduce yourself to this person and ask her what she wants to be able to do with what she learns today.*

- **Connection #8:** *Take thirty seconds to shake hands and welcome as many people around you as you can. Then take thirty more seconds to tell one new friend one important fact you already know about today's topic.*

- **Connection #9:** *Think of three things you already know about the topic and one thing you want to learn today. Introduce yourself to a person near you and tell this person what you thought of.*

- **Connection #10:** *In the next thirty seconds, on an index card, write one personal goal for this training, that is, what you want to walk away with, and write one fact you already know about the topic. Then take thirty seconds to share what you wrote with the person seated next to you.*

Tips and Variations!

The Power of the First Minute. Whenever possible, make the first minute or two of your training the connection time. Don't waste the powerfully memorable opening moments on housekeeping, introductory remarks, or goal-setting. You can get to those items after the Connection activity. Recognize and honor your learners first with a Connection activity—this gives them the message that the training is about them, not about you.

More Than One. You can do a Connection activity at the beginning of each major segment of a longer training, especially if you are covering different concepts each time. For example, if the training is about job retention, the first activity has learners talking about what makes a good employee. The second connection has learners discussing what needs to be on a résumé form. During the third connecting exercise, learners talk about job interview do's and don'ts.

Concepts Within Topics. Instead of sharing one fact they know about the topic, tell participants to share one fact they know about a specific topic-related concept. For example, if the training is about customer service, they can state one fact they know about handling a difficult customer.

Side to Side. Instead of connecting with the people sitting or standing closest to them, have participants on one side of the room (or at one table) stand and move to the other side (or to another table) and connect with the folks there.

Create Your Own!

In the box below, jot down your own Connection ideas.

Time Sponges

What Is a Time Sponge?

A Time Sponge is a short, topic-related activity that soaks up time that would normally be spent on nontraining things. Examples of these nontraining times include the few minutes before the opening, moments immediately after a coffee or lunch break, and whenever participants finish an activity early and have nothing else to do.

What Does a Time Sponge Do?

A time sponge gives those who are early arrivals, late arrivals, or who finish early something to do or talk about that is topic-related. There are three basic kinds of Time Sponges in this section:

- *Quick Start Sponges.* These activities soak up two or three minutes before the official opening. Or use one as an official opening activity to get people connected to each other and to the training topic.
- *Take a Break Sponges.* These exercises soak up a few minutes of break time for learners who want to continue working with the material or have nothing else to do. They also soak up the first minute or two after participants return from a coffee, bathroom, or lunch break.
- *Early to Finish Sponges.* These activities fill time when learners have completed a game or project and are waiting for others to finish.

A Sponge activity will

- *Focus* learners on the topic and what they already know or have learned about it.
- *Accommodate* both early and late arrivals.
- *Build* a safe, productive learning community.
- *Give* learners activity options during nontraining minutes.

- *Make* participants self-directed learners, that is, they choose a topic-related follow-up activity to do on their own. Because the Sponge activity instructions are posted where everyone can read them, learners can do the activity with no direct instruction or help from you.
- *Engage* learners' minds from the moment they enter the room.
- *Increase* the actual amount of training time that is content-related.
- *Review* material in interesting, thought-provoking ways.

 Getting Ready

Materials: Depending upon the activity, learners may need handouts, pens or pencils, broad-tipped felt pens, index cards, Post-it® notes, or chart paper taped to the walls. Read the specific Sponge activity to see what you will need.

Setup: Post the Sponge instructions where training participants can see them as soon as they enter the room. For small groups (fewer than twenty), print the instructions on chart paper and position the chart stand either by the door or in the front of the room. Chart printing needs to be large, made with broad-tipped felt pens, in dark colors, and visible from across the room. Or print the instructions on paper for each table group or on index cards placed on each chair. For larger groups, use a computer slide or overhead transparency. The room setup is not important as long as everyone can see the posted Sponge instructions. Participants may need enough space to move around the room for some activities.

Group Size: Any size group is fine.

Ten Quick Start Sponges

- **Quick Start #1:** *After reading this, introduce yourself to someone you don't know and ask that person to list three things he hopes to learn from the training.*
- **Quick Start #2:** *When you finish reading this, find someone who was born in the same birth season as you (spring, summer, fall, winter) and tell that person three things you already know about the topic.*

- **Quick Start #3:** *After reading this, stand and take a short survey by asking four other participants what they want to learn today. Be ready to state your survey results when asked to do so.*

- **Quick Start #4:** *On an index card, jot down two things you want to learn today. Then introduce yourself to someone seated near you and compare your lists.*

- **Quick Start #5:** *On your handout, write three facts you already know about the topic. Then stand and find another person who has completed her list and compare lists.*

- **Quick Start #6:** *Right now stand and introduce yourself to two other people. Ask them to tell you one topic-related issue that they have had to deal with.*

- **Quick Start #7:** *Right now, turn to someone seated near you and ask her to share a best practice she uses related to the training topic.*

- **Quick Start #8:** *During the next sixty seconds, stand and introduce yourself to a person standing near you. Tell him a topic-related question that you want answered. Be ready to state your partner's question when asked to do so.*

- **Quick Start #9:** *During the next sixty seconds, introduce yourself to one other person and tell her what you hope one of the training take-aways will be.*

- **Quick Start #10:** *During the next sixty seconds, shake hands (or smile and say hello) to at least six people in the room, and tell them why you are here.*

Ten Take a Break Sponges

- **Take a Break #1:** *During the break, ask three other people the following question: "What is the most important concept you've learned so far?"*

- **Take a Break #2:** *During the break, compare your notes with another person's notes. Jot down any additional facts from the other person's notes that you want to remember.*

- **Take a Break #3:** *When you return from the break, tell the person nearest you what you consider the most useful thing you've learned so far.*

- **Take a Break #4:** *When you return from the break, make up a question about what you've learned and see whether the person nearest you can answer your question.*

- **Take a Break #5:** *During the break, look over your written materials (or handouts) and circle three important ideas that you want to remember.*

- **Take a Break #6:** *When you return from the break, take sixty seconds to think about what you've learned so far. Jot down the best idea on a Post-it® note and stick it to this chart paper (or on a wall or door).*

- **Take a Break #7:** On the walls, post four or five charts with questions related to the topic, one question per chart. The Sponge instructions say: *Before the break is over, read the wall chart questions. Use a felt pen to write on the charts your response to one or more of the questions.*

- **Take a Break #8:** On a wall, hang a number of charts together and label them "Graffiti Wall." The Sponge instructions say: *Before the break is over, use a felt pen to jot down on the Graffiti Wall an opinion, comment, or question about the topic.*

- **Take a Break #9:** *Before you sit down, stretch your body and then tell another person standing near you what you like best about the training so far.*

- **Take a Break #10:** *Before you sit down, walk outside and take a few deep breaths of fresh air. Or walk around the room and stretch your large muscles: legs, back, arms, neck, shoulders.*

Ten Early to Finish Sponges

- **Early to Finish #1:** *When you are done, discuss with your table group (small group or another person) what you learned from the activity and what you plan to do with the new information.*

- **Early to Finish #2:** *When you are done, jot down the three (five, seven) most important things you learned from the activity. Compare your list with another person's list.*

- **Early to Finish #3:** *Finished early? Find one or two others who have finished early, too, and create a list of ways you can use the information. Use a felt pen to print your list on chart paper, and post it on a wall.*

- **Early to Finish #4:** On chart paper (or overhead or slide), list three questions pertaining to the longer activity. The Sponge instructions say: *When you finish the activity, write your answers on an index card to the three questions listed on the chart. Compare your answers to another person's answers who has finished early.*

- **Early to Finish #5:** *Finished early? Look over all your written materials, and make a list of the best ideas from the readings.*

- **Early to Finish #6:** *When you're done, take an index card and on one side write a question about the material and on the other side write the answer to your question. Then exchange cards with another person and see whether you can answer each other's questions correctly.*

- **Early to Finish #7:** *When you're done, think about what you've learned and make a list of the names of colleagues with whom you could share this information.*

- **Early to Finish #8:** Print a list of Early to Finish activity choices on a chart and post it where all training participants can see it. The list can include a number of these Early to Finish activities. The Sponge instructions say: *If you finish early, choose an activity from this list to do.*

- **Early to Finish #9:** *If you finish early, create a verbal metaphor for what you have learned (example: "What I've learned is like a bridge because. . . .") and be ready to share your metaphor with others who finish early, too.*

- **Early to Finish #10:** *If you finish early, observe the others who are still engaged in the activity. Ask them first whether they will be comfortable with you doing this.*

Tips and Variations!

Post Them. Before the training, create printed instructions for all the Sponge activities you plan to use. It's better to have a selection to choose from up front rather than stopping in the middle of the training to write the instructions. Post the written instructions where everyone can see them when the time comes to do the activities.

Tell Them. If you want all learners to do the Sponge activity, then say, "Please read the activity on the chart (slide, overhead), and take one minute to do it now." Or, "When you get back from the lunch break, please read and do the activity that is posted on the chart." Otherwise, some participants will see, read, and do the Sponge and some won't. This is an acceptable option also.

Talk About It. You can always process the Sponge activity by facilitating a one-minute, whole-group discussion about what the group learned. Or follow the activity with a sixty-second Shout Out of what they learned from the Sponge.

One per Table. If your learners are seated in table groups, print the Sponge instructions on pieces of colorful typing or construction paper and place one paper on each group's table.

Read and Pass. If your learners are seated in a theater-style room with chairs in rows and no tables, print the Sponge instructions on a few pieces of colorful typing or construction paper and direct learners to read and then pass the papers. The written Sponge instructions can begin with: When you read this, pass it on and then do the following . . .

Learner-Created Sponges. At the beginning of a lengthy training, explain to your participants what Sponges are, and then tell each table group to create a Sponge and write it on an index card. Collect the cards. Each time you use a Sponge, choose one from their cards.

Sponge Questions. When the training begins, ask participants to jot down questions they want answered on index cards. Collect the cards. Use their questions later as Sponges. Or post all the questions on a wall chart and direct participants to discuss and answer one each time they take a break.

Create Your Own!

In the box below, write your own Sponge ideas.

The Ten-Minute Trainer

Pair Shares

What Is a Pair Share?

Also called a Dyad Dialogue or a Neighbor Nudge, this
activity is the quickest, easiest, and psychologically the
safest way to invite learners to participate. During a Pair
Share, each learner turns to another person and engages
in a short discussion about something that is topic related.
With a Pair Share, learners don't have to worry about how
they will sound in front of their peers. Nor do learners
need to be concerned about whether or not they know the right answer. After all,
the only person they will be talking with will be the person seated next to them.

What Does a Pair Share Do?

A Pair Share helps learners

- *Review* information in an easy, quick, low-risk way.
- *Remember* what they just heard.
- *Connect* what they just heard with what they already know.
- *Connect* with each other in order to build a safe learning community.
- *Become* more comfortable with interaction and active involvement in the learning.

When learners participate in a Pair Share, expect to see them

- *Turn and talk* to someone they are sitting (or standing) next to.
- *Listen* as the other person is talking.
- *Become involved* in a discussion about the topic.
- *Feel more at ease* with you, with each other, and with the topic.
- *Be more willing* to ask questions.
- *Look more awake*, alert, and interested as you lecture.

 # Getting Ready

Materials: Extra materials are unnecessary.

Setup: Special setup is unnecessary.

Group Size: Any size group is fine.

Ten Pair Shares

- **Pair Share #1:** *Turn to your neighbor—the person sitting next to you—and tell him the most important fact you just learned in the last ten minutes.*

- **Pair Share #2:** *Turn to the person sitting behind you (across from you, in front of you) and ask her to summarize what she just learned in the last ten minutes.*

- **Pair Share #3:** *Turn to a person you haven't talked to yet and tell that person why you think the information you just heard is important to what you do.*

- **Pair Share #4:** *Make up a quick question about what you've just learned. See whether the person sitting next to you can answer your question.*

- **Pair Share #5:** *Ask the person seated across from you how what he just heard fits with what he already knew about the topic.*

- **Pair Share #6:** *Number off around your table (or down your row) into ones and twos. Ones, you have fifteen seconds to tell Twos the most important thing you just learned about the topic. Twos, you have fifteen seconds to tell Ones a way you can use the information you just learned.*

- **Pair Share #7:** *Together with your neighbor, create a phrase that summarizes what you've just learned. Be ready to tell the whole group the phrase when I ask you to do so.*

- **Pair Share #8:** *With your neighbor, create a question about what you've just learned. Be sure to write down the question so that we can come back to it later.*

- **Pair Share #9:** *With your neighbor, identify one problem, concern, or issue related to what you just learned.*

- **Pair Share #10:** *Tell your neighbor the answer to a question related to what you just learned. See whether she can figure out the question that goes with the answer.*

Tips and Variations!

Sit or Stand. If learners have been sitting awhile, direct them to stand up before doing the Pair Share.

Triads Are OK. Tell learners to do the activity in pairs or triads so that no one is left out.

Talk or Not. If you have the time, or feel it is important enough, you can lead a short, whole-group discussion about the Pair Share responses. Ask for volunteers to tell the group what they discussed in pairs. To do this activity processing, or not, is your call.

Hair-Pair Share. Tell learners to pair up and figure out who has the shortest hair and who has the longest hair. Then say, "Short Hair, ask Long Hair a question about what you just learned. If Long Hair can answer the question, give him or her a thumbs up." Or, "Long Hair, ask Short Hair to explain a term you just learned. If correct, give him or her a high-five." A caveat: be cautious about using characteristics that imply gender, ethnicity, or cultural biases or that could make people uncomfortable, such as weight or size.

Use Shoes. Instead of hair, tell pairs to discover who has the newest or oldest shoes, the longest or shortest middle name, the greater or fewer number of siblings, or anything else that will add a note of levity and community-building while reviewing the information.

Pair Share Plus One. Combine a Pair Share with any other sixty-second activity to deepen the learning. For example, after doing the Pair Share, learners may do a Shout Out, with a few of them stating aloud what they said to their partners. Or they might do a Think and Write, jotting down what they learned from the Pair Share. Read through all the activities in Part One so that you can choose which ones to combine.

Create Your Own!

Use the box below to list your own Pair Share ideas.

Shout Outs

What Is a Shout Out?

A Shout Out is an activity that encourages learners to state what they already know or have learned by responding to a topic-related question or comment from you. A Shout Out makes the whole group responsible for the number of responses needed. It also increases learner involvement, as well as critical thinking skills, because learners need to come up with more than one right answer. Participants don't really have to shout—they can use normal voices to respond, as per your instructions.

The Shout Out is one of the most versatile sixty-second activities around. Experiment with it to make it work for you and your learners. As an interactive lecture technique, it's tops!

What Does a Shout Out Do?

A Shout Out is a quick way to

- *Elicit* verbal responses from a group of learners.
- *Structure* learners' statements so that they say a specific type of response (facts, questions, answers, words, phrases) or a specific number of responses.
- *Make* the group responsible for thinking up the answers to a topic-related question.
- *Involve* more learners so that the same people aren't always answering the questions.
- *Increase* critical thinking about the topic by eliciting a certain number of "right" answers from the group.
- *Validate* what the learners already know about the topic.
- *Transform* a lecture from a monologue into a dialogue.

- *Eliminate* the total silence that follows when you say, "Are there any questions?"
- *Check* for understanding (if you see a lot of blank stares, you know that you need to reteach the information).

 # Getting Ready

Materials: No special materials are needed.

Setup: No special room arrangement or setup is necessary.

Group Size: Any size group is fine.

Ten Shout Outs

- **Shout Out #1:** *Shout out a number between one and ten. Now tell me* (state the number) *facts you already know about the topic.*
- **Shout Out #2:** *Shout out six things you want to learn from this training.*
- **Shout Out #3:** *Tell me three topic-related issues that are really important to you right now.*
- **Shout Out #4:** *Shout out four ways you can use the information we've covered so far.*
- **Shout Out #5:** *With the person next to you, make up a question related to what you've been learning. Let's hear three of those questions.*
- **Shout Out #6:** *Think of a word or phrase that summarizes what you've learned so far. On the count of three, everyone shout out his or her word.*
- **Shout Out #7:** Ask the group a question. Then say: *We need five answers to this question.*
- **Shout Out #8:** *Tell me ten things you have learned today that you didn't know before.*
- **Shout Out #9:** *Let's hear seven ways that you can use what you've learned today.*
- **Shout Out #10:** Post a list of important, topic-related words or terms. Say: *When I point to the word, everyone shout it out. Then turn to the person next to you and take turns defining the word for each other.*

Tips and Variations !

Group Number. As with Shout Out #1, the whole group can choose the number of statements to shout out. Or tell group members to choose a number between two other numbers. If the number they choose is too low or too high, have them choose again with some direction from you.

Instructor-Led Number. As with Shout Out #2, tell the learners how many facts about the topic or answers to the question they need to state.

Instructor-Led Beginning. Begin the Shout Out by stating the first fact. As learners shout out the other facts, keep track of the numbers (*That's one; that's two; we need three more.*).

Add to It. After learners have shouted out their facts about the topic or answers to your question, add information that the learners didn't state.

All Answers Are OK. Like any brainstorming activity, accept *all* answers during a Shout Out. After each answer, simply say, *Yes or That's [number]*, or *Great—let's have another one*. If the answer is incorrect, say, *Hold that thought and we'll come back to it*, and go on with the Shout Out. Address any misconceptions when the Shout Out is over.

Affirm the Learners. At the end of the Shout Out, thank the learners and continue with the lesson.

Small Group Shout Out. If learners are in small groups, direct one small group to state a certain number of topic-related facts.

From Small to Large. Tell all small groups to work together first to gather a specific number of facts. Then direct them to take turns stating one fact from their small group discussion.

Shout and Write. Learners verbally state a number of questions about the topic. A volunteer writes the questions on a chart for discussion later.

Say and Sing. If you have a specific, topic-related sentence, acronym, rhyme, or jingle you want your learners to memorize, post it where they can see it. Periodically have them join you in shouting it out, whispering it, singing it, or saying it.

Openings and Closings. Use the Shout Out at the beginning of your training as another kind of connecting activity. Or use it at the closing of your training to review what was learned.

Create Your Own!

Write more Shout Out ideas here.

Think and Write

What Is a Think and Write?

During this activity, learners take a moment to think about what they have learned and then write down their thoughts, as per your instructions. The Think and Write is more introspective than other sixty-second activities because learners quietly reflect upon what they learned. Corporate training guru Dr. Sivasailam "Thiagi" Thiagarajan (*Design Your Own Games and Activities*, 2003) calls this "Rapid Reflection" time. Whatever you choose to call it, use it to help learners mentally absorb the training material.

What Does a Think and Write Do?

With one minute of quiet reflection and writing, learners can

- *Deepen* their own understanding of the concepts learned.
- *Link* what they are learning with what they already know.
- *Experience* a moment of quiet energy as they reflect on what they've learned.
- *Discover* what they may still have a question about.
- *Relax* and take a break from interacting with other learners.
- *Begin* to internalize the information they are learning.
- *Move* the information more into long-term memory.

Getting Ready

Materials: Depending upon the activity, learners will need handouts, scratch paper, pens or pencils, index cards, Post-it® notes, and wall charts (for the Post-it® notes). Read the specific activity to see what you will need.

Setup: No special room setup is required.

Group Size: Any size group is fine.

Ten Think and Write Activities

- **Think and Write #1:** *Think about the material we've just covered. Write one sentence that summarizes this information.*

- **Think and Write #2:** *Think about what you've just learned. If you had to explain the main idea to someone else, what would you say? Write your explanation in a sentence or two.*

- **Think and Write #3:** *Think about how you can use this information. Jot down two or three ways you could apply what you've learned.*

- **Think and Write #4:** *Think about a question you still have concerning this information. Write your question on an index card and pass it up to me. If you don't have a question, jot down the most important thing you've learned so far.*

- **Think and Write #5:** Post a list of topic-related terms that you've lectured about. Then say: *Look over these terms. Choose one and write a sentence defining it.*

- **Think and Write #6:** *Think about an action plan for using this information. Write down your action plan. If you have time, quietly share it with the person next to you.*

- **Think and Write #7:** Point to a wall chart titled "Test Questions." Say: *If you had to create a test about the material you've learned, what would be a test question you would include? Write it down on a Post-it® note and stick it on the wall chart.*

- **Think and Write #8:** *On an index card, write down a test question related to this material. Write the answer to the question on the back of the card. Now exchange cards with someone next to you, making sure the question side is up. Write the answer to the question you just received and then check the back of the card to see whether your answer is correct.*

- **Think and Write #9:** *Who are three people you could share this information with? Jot down their names and what you would tell them on your handout.*
- **Think and Write #10:** *Think about a problem related to this topic. Jot it down in a sentence or two. Later I'll ask for a few volunteers to share their written problems with us and we'll brainstorm some solutions.*

¡ Tips and Variations !

Change the Time. Observe the group. If most learners finish before the minute is up, stop the activity. If most are still writing when the minute is up, give them additional time to finish.

Add a Pair Share. If desired, follow the Think and Write with a Pair Share so that learners can quietly listen to each other's ideas.

From Noisy to Quiet. Use a Think and Write to quiet the group after a physically active, high-energy activity.

Sit and Stretch. Direct learners to stretch while seated before doing the activity.

Stand and Stretch. Have learners stand and stretch while thinking and then sit back down to write.

Create Your Own!

Jot down your own Think and Write ideas in the box below.

Signals

What Is a Signal?

A Signal is a hand or body motion, or a choral response, used by learners to answer a question or demonstrate their understanding of a concept. One of the most widely used Signals trainers tell participants to use is "Raise your hand if . . ." followed by a topic-related statement. But Signals can be unusual sounds and motions, too. They can also be learner-created. Signals involve all learners and add a kinesthetic element to a lecture.

What Does a Signal Do?

Signals help you, the trainer, to

- *Check* your learners' understanding of important material.
- *Decide* what, if anything, to reteach.
- *Add* a small degree of levity to your lecture.
- *Involve* your learners in your lecture without sacrificing time or informational flow.

Signals also help the learners to

- *Remain* awake and involved in the lecture.
- *Think* about what they've heard.
- *Make* some opinion-based decisions about what they've learned.
- *Interact* with the new information in quick, low-risk ways.
- *Stay* focused on material being presented.

Getting Ready

Materials: Depending upon the activity, learners will need index cards, pens or pencils, and small, individual noisemakers—one item each per person. Read the specific Signal activity to see what you will need.

Setup: A special room setup is unnecessary.

Group Size: Any size group is fine.

Ten Signals

- **Signal #1:** *When I ask you a yes or no question, show me thumbs up for yes and thumbs down for no.*

- **Signal #2:** *If you want me to repeat certain information, show me this sign.* (Circle your hand above your head and tell participants to do it with you.)

- **Signal #3:** *When I make a statement related to the topic, clap your hands if you agree with the statement and stomp your feet if you don't agree.*

- **Signal #4:** *Take an index card and print in large letters "True" on one side and "False" on the other side. When I make a statement related to what you have been learning, hold up the card with your answer facing me so that I can see whether you think the statement is true or false.*

- **Signal #5:** *Stand up if you believe that this statement is a fact* (read a statement about what they have been learning). Give learners the answer, and acknowledge those who were correct. Then direct the standing people to sit, and do the Signal again with another statement.

- **Signal #6:** *I am going to ask you a question about the material we've covered. Stand if you're pretty sure you can answer the question correctly. Remain seated if you're not sure, or if you want more time to think about it. Standing people, please share your answer with the seated people.*

- **Signal #7:** *Let me hear a "Way cool!" if you agree. Let me hear a "No way!" if you disagree.*

- **Signal #8:** *Sound your noisemaker if you agree. Or, Sound your noisemaker if you think this is a good idea. Or, Sound your noisemaker if you have another idea to go along with what we've just talked about.*

- **Signal #9:** *Write your answer to this question on a piece of paper. Wave your paper in the air to show me that you're ready to read it to the group.* (Have a few volunteers read their answers.)

- **Signal #10:** *On a scale of one to five, one means that you need more clarification about this concept. Five means that you've got it and are ready to move on. Show me by holding up your fingers where you are on the one-to-five scale.*

Tips and Variations!

Check It Out. Watch learners' signals to get a feeling for whether they really understand the material. If you get several wrong answers, you don't even need to point that out—you just need to reteach that material.

More Body and Voice Signals. Signals can also include a topic-related phrase that learners verbally repeat, a topic-related motion, the chorus of a song, a line of poetry, nodding or shaking of heads, slapping the table tops, whole-body motion (swaying, dancing, the "cool wave" done in sports stadiums), finger-snapping, or anything you can think of that is short, fun, and that engages learners in kinesthetic ways.

Learner-Created Signals. For a lengthy training, give learners time to make up their own signals. Have them teach their signals to the whole group, then use those signals during the training.

Noisemaker Signals. Pass out small, individual noisemakers and have learners use them periodically in place of hand signals.

Thematic Signals. If you have a training theme (for example, solving a mystery, a baseball game, visiting a tropical island, the circus), make up signals that are theme related.

Create Your Own!

Create your own Signals in the box below.

Doodles

What Is a Doodle?

With sixty-second Doodles, learners simply create images—icons, lines, shapes, drawings, cartoons, symbols, stick figures, or logos—to represent a topic-related fact or concept.

If the word *doodle* frightens *(I don't know how to draw!)* or offends some learners *(Doodling is for kids—I don't doodle!)*, call the activity by another name. Visual Analog will do, since a doodle is a visual analogy, that is, an image that represents a concept. Or call it a Sixty-Second Graphic or a Topic Icon for technology folks in the group.

A Doodle is a right-brain activity, since humans process images in the right hemisphere of the cerebrum or thinking brain. Read "What's a Picture Worth?" in Part Three to find out more about the power of images in learning.

What Does a Doodle Do? (Doodlee-Do!)

Creating images to represent concepts is one of the most powerful ways of moving information from short-term to long-term memory. With a Doodle, you enable learners to

- *Use* both hemispheres of their thinking brain to learn.
- *Remember* information longer than they would if they just listened to a lecture and then wrote down words.
- *Begin* to move learning into long-term memory.
- *Take* a right-brain (visual or picture-based) break from left-brain (linguistic or word-based) material.
- *Represent* concepts in a more interesting, creative way.

- *Have* a little fun with the learning, thereby creating an "endorphin release" of pleasure chemicals in the brain.
- *Deepen* their understanding of the material by representing it with another medium.
- *Access* the power of the visual image.

Getting Ready

Materials: Depending upon the activity, learners will need handouts as well as drawing materials such as Post-it® notes, blank colored paper, thin or broad-tipped colored felt pens, scratch paper, pens or pencils, and index cards. Read the specific activity to see what you will need.

Setup: A special room setup is unnecessary.

Group Size: Any size group is fine.

Ten Doodles

- **Doodle #1:** *Draw a doodle representing the most important thing you've just learned. Your doodle can be a line, a shape, a squiggle, an icon, a cartoon, a symbol, or anything visual. Explain your doodle to the person sitting next to you.*
- **Doodle #2:** *Draw a line that stands for one fact from the material we've covered. Your line can be a certain shape, a squiggle, the arrows of a flow chart, or a series of lines that go together in some way. Explain your line to the person in front or behind you.*
- **Doodle #3:** *Create a simple logo representing the topic. Explain your logo to your table group.*
- **Doodle #4:** *Think of an image that will help you remember this fact. Draw a doodle of that image.*
- **Doodle #5:** *Draw a geometric shape to represent this concept. Explain your drawing to your neighbor.*
- **Doodle #6:** *I am going to represent this concept with an image. As I draw it, you draw it with me.*

- **Doodle #7:** *Write down the three most important concepts we've talked about so far. Draw an image to represent each concept. Then draw lines or squiggles to represent the connections between the images.*
- **Doodle #8:** *Draw one cartoon or icon for each important concept. Label your icons.*
- **Doodle #9:** *Choose six key words from the material we've covered. Write the words on a piece of paper, then draw a doodle representing each word.*
- **Doodle #10:** *Draw a picture that represents an important fact from the information we've just covered and show your drawing to your neighbor. See whether your neighbor can figure out what your picture represents without your having to tell him. Let him know whether he got it right.*

¡Tips and Variations!

You First. When you tell learners to draw a doodle, model what you want them to do by drawing a sample doodle on chart paper or an overhead transparency. Some learners will draw what you draw; others will make up their own doodles. You can also make a point of asking them to copy your doodle, especially if you have specific images you want them to associate with the concepts.

Remember This. Have learners create doodles only for the important facts that you want them to remember. For example, if you're teaching a company safety class, you might have learners draw doodles representing the steps to take when using a fire extinguisher. But you wouldn't have them doodle information they don't need to remember, such as all the chemical names in the hazardous materials binder.

Note-Taking Doodles. Create a note-taking page for participants before the training begins. Include blank spaces for doodling. Use the Graphic Organizers in "What's a Picture Worth?" in Part Three for this purpose.

Post-it® Doodles. Learners can doodle on Post-it® notes and stick them on a wall chart.

Collage Doodles. Tell learners to use colored paper to make a "doodle collage" of all their topic-related images. They may label the images if they wish.

Thought Doodles. Encourage learners to think in pictures by asking them: *What image comes to mind when you think of . . .?*

Group-Created Doodles. Learners work together in pairs, triads, or small groups to create visual images of what they learned.

Metaphoric Doodles. Learners make up metaphors for certain concepts and then draw and share the metaphors. Read "Metaphor Magic!" later in Part One for more ideas.

Create Your Own!

In the box below, doodle your own Doodle ideas.

Pop-Ups

What Is a Pop-Up?

A Pop-Up is a kinesthetic activity that increases physical energy while learners review material. With a Pop-Up, a few or all of the learners stand up or sit down, as per your instructions. While standing, they discuss what you direct them to talk about. With some Pop-Ups, all learners stand all at once. With others, learners literally pop out of their chairs in a rapid-fire fashion, one at a time, to make topic-related statements. You can add a little competition to the mix if you wish.

What Does a Pop-Up Do?

With a Pop-Up, learners will

- *Stand* while responding to a question or comment from you.
- *Increase* their own physical energy while talking.
- *Link* what they are learning to what they already know.
- *Enjoy* a little friendly competition that makes the activity feel different from other review strategies.
- *Think*—literally—on their feet, standing and sitting quickly.

For strong kinesthetic learners—those who need to move their bodies while learning—a Pop-Up is a lifesaver.

 Getting Ready

Materials: Depending upon the activity, you may need topic-related questions that you have already written on chart paper (or an overhead transparency or computer slide), small prizes or activity souvenirs, and a watch with a sweep hand for counting the seconds. Read the specific activity to see what you will need.

Setup: Learners will need enough space around them to be able to stand up and sit down without bumping into other people or furniture.

Group Size: Any size group is fine.

Ten Pop-Ups

- **Pop-Up #1:** Post a topic-related question on a chart, overhead, or computer slide. Then say: *The last person in your table group (or row) to pop out of his chair answers this question for your group. Your group will let him know if his answer is correct.*

- **Pop-Up #2:** Post a question on a chart, overhead, or computer slide. Then say: *The first person in your table group (or row) to pop out of her chair chooses the group member to answer this question. The group will let this person know if the answer is correct.*

- **Pop-Up #3:** Post a list of topic-related terms on a chart, overhead, or computer slide. Then say: *The first six people in the room to pop up and define six of these terms for us each get to take home a souvenir.* Give each a small prize or souvenir and thank them as they do this.

- **Pop-Up #4:** Direct the whole group to stand up. Then say: *To earn your chair back, you need to tell your table group (standing group or row) how you plan to use what you have learned. When you have done this, you may sit back down.*

- **Pop-Up #5:** *The last person to pop out of his chair has to explain to the whole group how he plans to use what he has learned.*

- **Pop-Up #6:** Assign a Timer and a Pop-Up Counter in the group. Then say: *A Pop-Up is when a person pops out of her chair and states the most important thing she has learned so far. In order to take our break, we need to have twenty Pop-Ups from the group in the next sixty seconds. Time begins now.*

- **Pop-Up #7:** Assign a Timer and a Pop-Up Counter in the group. Then say: *A Pop-Up is when a person pops out of his chair and states what he plans to do with what he has learned this morning. In order to get three (or five) extra lunchtime minutes, we need to have fifteen Pop-Ups from the group in the next sixty seconds. Time begins now.*

- **Pop-Up #8:** *Stand up and tell the person standing next to you three important things you just learned. Sit down when you have finished.*

- **Pop-Up #9:** *The last person in your table group (or row) to pop out of his chair has to ask your group a content-related question that can't have a simple yes or no answer. The Pop-Up person needs to know the answer to his own question and needs to tell his group whether or not they answered the question correctly.*

- **Pop-Up #10:** *Stand up and ask the person standing next to you a question about the material we've covered. Sit back down when that person has finished answering the question to your satisfaction.*

i Tips and Variations *!*

Safe Enough to Move. Make sure it is physically safe for learners to stand and sit quickly (for example, enough space around furniture, no protruding objects around that would endanger anyone).

Timer and Counter. Assign a training participant to be your Pop-Up Timer and another to be the Pop-Up Counter. These responsibilities increase learner involvement and leadership.

Stick to the Time. Stick to the sixty seconds, since timing, in this case, is an important part of the friendly competition.

It's Your Call. With a little experimentation, you will find a happy medium between the number of responses needed and the time it takes to state them, thus making the activity challenging but doable. Usually, fewer than fifteen responses in sixty seconds are too few, and over thirty may be too many. It's your judgment call.

Group Applause. Encourage participants to applaud themselves if they beat the Pop-Up time, thereby acknowledging the group effort and ending the activity on a high-energy note.

Pop-Up Prizes. With small groups or table groups, have each group do as many Pop-Ups as it can in sixty seconds. The group with the greatest number of Pop-Ups receives small prizes, or a round of applause.

Beat the Record. Instead of your setting a specific number of Pop-Ups for the whole group, learners see how many they can do as a group in sixty seconds. Then, during a second round of Pop-Ups later, learners try to beat their own score by doing more Pop-Ups than they did during the first round.

Learner-Created Topic. Encourage participants to decide what the topic of the Pop-Up will be.

Learner-Created Pop-Ups. For a lengthy training, learners make up a posted list of topic-related concepts and questions. Then, every time you decide to do a Pop-Up, choose a question or topic from the list.

Sound or Motion Pop-Ups. Participants stand up and make a sound or do a motion representing the main idea or a topic-related fact.

Last Person In. Before a break, announce that the last person to return to the training room after the break has to stand up and tell the whole group the three most important things he has learned so far. Or announce that the last five people to return have to create a logo, slogan, or doodle representing the most important thing they learned. Later they stand and share their creation with the whole group.

Create Your Own!

Brainstorm your own Pop-Up ideas in the box below.

Mark-Ups

What Is a Mark-Up?

A Mark-Up is an activity in which you instruct learners to mark their written material in certain ways so that they will remember the information longer. Use a Mark-Up whenever you include written items—handouts, textbooks, worksheets, binders, and the like—to supplement your training.

According to educational research, most learners only remember about 10 percent of what they read. If they interact with the written information in some way, the probability increases that learners will remember more of what they read. And since a Mark-Up is kinesthetic—that is, it requires movement—participants who learn through doing will find it easier to pay attention when listening to a lecture.

What Does a Mark-Up Do?

With a Mark-Up, learners will

- *Remain* focused on the written material in front of them.
- *Think* about the information as they read it.
- *Analyze* the new information while reading it.
- *Make* the written material more meaningful and memorable.
- *Find* the written key points more quickly after the training is over.
- *Review* written information more easily later.

Getting Ready

Materials: In addition to the written materials (handouts, workbooks, textbooks, worksheets—whatever training materials you use), learners will also need pens or pencils, highlighters, and small stickers or sticky dots (the latter two items are optional but add a measure of color and fun to the printed information). Read the specific activity to see what is needed.

Setup: A special room setup is unnecessary.

Group Size: Any size group is fine.

Ten Mark-Ups

- **Mark-Up #1:** *Draw a square (a circle) around this important word (words, phrases).*

- **Mark-Up #2:** *Cross out the least important sentence on this page.*

- **Mark-Up #3:** *Connect this word (words, phrase) to that word with a line or arrow.*

- **Mark-Up #4:** *Put a star or check mark (sticker or dot) in front of this item (sentence, bulleted point).*

- **Mark-Up #5:** *Underline (or highlight) the main idea in this sentence (or the most meaningful words in this section).*

- **Mark-Up #6:** If you've created a "fill-it in" worksheet, say: *As I lecture, fill in the words that are missing on this page.* Or tell learners what to write in the blank spaces.

- **Mark-Up #7:** *Quickly read the bulleted items on this page. Circle (or put a dot or sticker beside) the three that are the most important (the most meaningful, the most useful) to you.*

- **Mark-Up #8:** *Silently skim this section. Draw a question mark beside any sentence that you have a question about or that you want more clarification about.*

- **Mark-Up #9:** *Write the words "I will use this" ("I will remember this," "This is a wow") beside three ideas on this page.*

- **Mark-Up #10:** *On this page, write the words "I agree" or "I disagree" beside each paragraph. Or write "Useful" or "Not Useful" beside the information.*

¡Tips and Variations!

Fill It In. If you want learners to write down key points or important words from your lecture, create a worksheet with blanks where the major points should be. As you cover the material, direct learners to fill in the blanks.

Cooperative Mark-Ups. Learners work in pairs or triads to decide what important information to highlight or underline.

Group-Directed Mark-Ups. Assign each small group a certain page or section of the written material. They read, discuss, and agree on what the most important points are. A spokesperson from each small group instructs the other groups to highlight or mark the information his group selected. Extend the Mark-Ups' time in order to do this.

Survey the Mark-Ups. Each person marks the most important words (phrases, sentences) in a section of reading material. Then all learners stand and take a quick survey by walking around the room and comparing what they marked to see whether most are in agreement.

Create Your Own!

In the box below, list your own Mark-Up ideas.

Tickets Out

What Is a Ticket Out?

A Ticket Out (also called an Exit Slip) is a written comment or verbal statement from the learners about what they have learned, what parts of the information are still confusing to them, a question they may still have, or what they consider to be the most important concept or main idea from the material presented. If you really want to make sure your learners understand the information you're teaching them, ask them to hand you a Ticket Out as they walk out the door for a break, for lunch, or at the end of the day. Or use a Ticket Out as an evaluation tool for part of the closing activities.

What Does a Ticket Out Do?

A Ticket Out helps you, the trainer, to

- *Check* for understanding, that is, find out what material is most or least understood.
- *Decide* what material you may need to reteach.
- *Answer* questions that learners may not feel comfortable asking in front of the whole group.
- *Get* a feeling for where your learners are both intellectually and emotionally in the training.
- *Know* whether you're on track or not with both the information and the learning needs of the participants.

A Ticket Out gives learners an opportunity to

- *Assess* their own understanding of what they have learned.

- *Ask* questions or make comments about the material anonymously in case they are shy about doing so in front of the whole group.
- *Decide* what has been most important to them.
- *Become* aware of any confusion that they may be feeling.
- *Give* the trainer honest feedback about the training.

 Getting Ready

Materials: Depending upon the activity, learners will need pens or pencils, broad-tipped colored felt pens, index cards, blank typing paper, Post-it® notes (one of each item per person), wall charts (for the Post-it® notes and the Graffiti Wall), and a small bag or box (one per table group or one by the door). Read the specific Ticket Out activity to see what you will need.

Setup: Any room setup will do.

Group Size: Any size group is fine.

Ten Tickets Out

- **Ticket Out #1:** Hang a chart paper labeled "Wow!" near the door. Say: *On a Post-it® note, write the most important thing you've learned so far, and stick the note on the "Wow!" wall chart on your way out the door.*

- **Ticket Out #2:** Hang a chart paper labeled "How About?" near the door. Say: *On a Post-it® note, write a question you want answered, and stick the note on the "How About?" wall chart on your way out the door.*

- **Ticket Out #3:** Stand by the training room door and say: *On an index card, write down three main ideas from the material we've covered, and hand the card to me on your way out.*

- **Ticket Out #4:** Stand by the training room door and say: *On an index card, write down what you want more clarification about, or a question you want answered, and hand the card to me before you leave.*

- **Ticket Out #5:** Have a small, colorful bag or box at each table group. Say: *On an index card, write a one-sentence opinion about an issue related to what you've learned, and drop it in the bag (box) before you leave.*

- **Ticket Out #6:** Stand by the door and say: *As you leave, please tell me a word or phrase that sums up your feelings about what you're learning so far.*

- **Ticket Out #7:** Stand by the door and say: *As you leave, please tell me one idea you plan to put to use after this training is over.*

- **Ticket Out #8:** Hang two or three chart papers labeled "Graffiti Wall" near the door. Say: *Before you leave the room, please take a felt pen and jot down on our Graffiti Wall your thoughts, feelings, opinions, or questions about the material we've covered so far.*

- **Ticket Out #9:** Place a small, colorful bag or box near the door. Say: *Before you leave, take an index card and write down a topic-related issue, question, or concern that you want addressed when we return. Drop your card in the bag (box) by the door.*

- **Ticket Out #10:** Place a chair by the door. Post a chart where everyone can see it with the following printed on it: "Glows and Grows." Say: *Please take a blank piece of typing paper and write the words "Glows and Grows" on it. A Glow is something that is working well for you in this training. A Grow is a question you want answered or a suggestion to make the training work even better. Please write your responses (you do not need to sign the paper) and place the paper on the chair by the door as you leave.*

¡Tips and Variations!

Before the Break. Do the Ticket Out activity sixty seconds before the break begins or the training ends in order to give learners time to complete it.

Read Them. At some point during the break or later in the day, privately read the Tickets Out so that you can address questions, concerns, and so forth. You can also give the whole group a verbal summary of their Tickets Out.

Q & A Time. Set aside time for a whole group question-and-answer session in which you read learners' Ticket Out questions and facilitate a discussion about the answers.

Change Your Agenda. Be ready to adjust your training agenda or objectives according to the feedback you receive.

Learner to Learner. Learners tell each other their Tickets Out, instead of reporting to you. Or learners write a note to a friend, telling the friend what they learned.

Pass Them Back. During the break, gather up the Ticket Out question cards or Post-it® notes. After the break, pass them out to the table groups or small group clusters and have the groups prepare answers to the questions. They report their answers to the whole group.

Choose One. Post a choice of two or three types of Tickets Out listed in this chapter on a wall chart. Direct learners to individually choose the Ticket Out they wish to do before they leave the room.

Posted Question. Post a topic-related question that learners need to answer either verbally or in writing before they leave the room.

Posted Issue. Post an issue related to the topic that learners need to begin discussing before they leave the room. Ask them to continue the discussion during the break and then hold a whole-group discussion about the issue when they return.

Posted Terms. Post a list of topic-related terms and have learners define or give an example of one term either verbally or in writing before they leave the room.

Create Your Own!

Can you think of other Ticket Out ideas? Write them here.

Action Plans

What Is an Action Plan?

An Action Plan is a participant's verbal or written commitment to do something with what he learned. It is an activity that encourages learners to think about the learning and to use it in some way after the training is over. An Action Plan also helps participants evaluate the training by thinking about what they've accomplished and how it matches up with their training goals, that is, what they wanted to learn.

An Action Plan is an important part of the Training Map (see "Mapping Your Message" in Part Two). Include Action Plans as closing activities or at the end of a training's major segments.

What Does a Sixty-Second Action Plan Do?

By making an Action Plan, learners will

- *Review* what they have learned and what they feel is really important to them.
- *Remember* their personal learning goals from the beginning of the training.
- *Evaluate* whether or not these goals have been met.
- *Decide* upon a course of action to take with what they have learned.
- *Make* a commitment to follow this course of action.
- *Apply* what they have learned to real-life experiences.
- *Realize* that true learning involves doing something with what they have learned.

 Getting Ready

Materials: Depending upon the activity, learners will need index cards, pens or pencils, Post-it® notes, blank postcards, and felt pens (one of each item per person). You will also need chart paper, tape, and a soft, throwable object such as a Koosh® or Nerf® ball. For Action Plans #6 and #7, you will need to prepare the charts beforehand, as directed. Read the specific Action Plan activity to see what is needed.

Setup: A special room setup is unnecessary.

Group Size: Any size group is fine.

Ten Action Plans

- **Action Plan #1:** *Turn to the person seated closest to you and finish this sentence: "I plan to . . ." by telling this person what you plan to do with what you learned today. Make sure no one is left out.*

- **Action Plan #2:** *Tell your table group members one of your training goals, how well this training met that goal, and what your next step is.*

- **Action Plan #3:** *What are three things you plan to do with what you learned? Tell three people around you what you are making a commitment to do when the training is over, and how you will judge your own success in completing these plans.*

- **Action Plan #4:** *On an index card, jot down two things you are going to do with this new information. Now compare your card with a neighbor's to see whether your action plans are the same or different.*

- **Action Plan #5:** *Take fifteen seconds to stand and find two people in the room who have not been your partners in any activity before.* Wait. *Now each take ten seconds to state what you plan to do with what you've learned today.* Wait. *Take the last fifteen seconds to shake hands and wish them luck with their action goals.*

- **Action Plan #6:** Tape from two to four wall charts close to the exit door. Print the words "Action Plans" in large, bold letters on them. Say: *With a felt pen, print your action plan, that is, what you plan to do with what you learned, on one of the wall charts marked "Action Plans." Make sure your printing is big and legible enough for people to read.* When participants get ready to walk out the door, direct them to read a couple of the action plans on the charts before they leave.

- **Action Plan #7:** Tape one to two wall charts close to the exit door. Print the words "Action Plans" in large, bold letters on them. Say: *On a Post-it® note,* *write these three words: "I plan to. . . ." Now finish the sentence by writing what you plan to do with what you've learned here today. On your way out of the room, stick your Action Plan to the wall chart by the door.*

- **Action Plan #8:** Have the whole group stand and do a ball toss (tossing any soft, throwable object from one person to another). Whoever catches the ball states her action plan and then tosses the ball to someone else. Keep the toss going for about a minute, or longer if you wish.

- **Action Plan #9:** *Think of a way you can hold yourself accountable for using what you've learned in this training. Tell a person near you what you thought of.*

- **Action Plan #10:** *On the front of a postcard, write what you plan to do with what you learned today, and some words of encouragement for yourself. On the back of the card, legibly print your name and mailing address. On your way out the door, please give the card to me. In two weeks, I will mail it back to you reminding you of the commitment to action that you made here today.* Collect the cards and two weeks later, stamp and mail them to the participants.

¡ Tips and Variations !

Make Them Specific. Direct learners to be as specific as possible by using concrete behaviors as their action plans. For example, for a technology training, they might say, *I will remember to run the virus protection program before going online*, instead of simply stating, *I will use this information tomorrow.*

Other Sixty-Second Action Plans. With small changes in instructions, many of the other activities in Part One can also be Action Plans. For example, use a Ticket Out, a Pair Share, or a Shout Out as part of the closing activities. Learners finish the sentence "I plan to . . ." during these activities.

Action Plan Worksheet. Create a worksheet dedicated to Action Plans. At various times in the training, refer learners to the worksheet and give them time to write down what they plan to do with the information they just learned. Use one of the Graphic Organizers at the end of "What's a Picture Worth?" in Part Three for this purpose.

Process the Action Plan. If you have a few extra minutes, ask for volunteers to state their action plans aloud. By doing this, participants can learn from hearing how other participants plan to use the training material.

Round Robin. If the group is small enough (a dozen or less), do a Round Robin Action Plan where the whole group stands in a circle and each states his action plan verbally until all have had a chance to do so.

Celebrate It. If time allows, combine an Action Plan activity with a sixty-second Celebration to end on a focused yet high-energy note.

Create Your Own!

Create more Action Plan ideas in the box below.

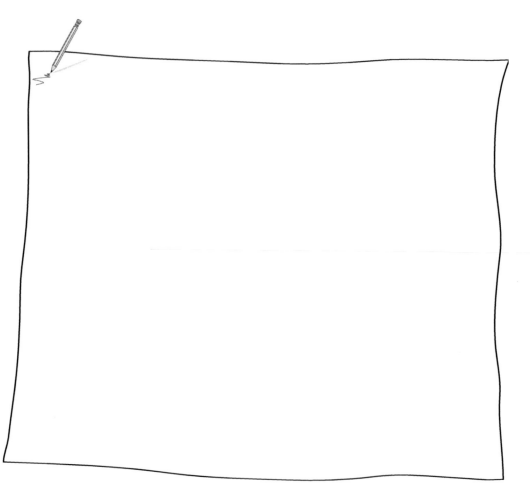

Celebrations

What Is a Celebration?

A Celebration is a closing activity that ends the training on a positive note, often with a burst of energy and enthusiasm. Like a Connection activity at the beginning of a training, a Celebration connects learners to each other once again at the end of the training. The Celebration ensures that training participants leave feeling good about what they learned and the learning community they shared.

The Celebration should be the last thing learners do before they leave the training room. If you include a training evaluation or final comments, do them before the Celebration activity. Why? Because the last minute or so of a training is a powerful time to reinforce both the learning and the learning community. When participants leave feeling good about themselves and the learning experience, they will seek out more of the same. The probability that they will become lifelong learners increases because of the positive feelings they have when they walk out the door.

What Does a Celebration Do?

With a sixty-second Celebration, you can

- *Create* a burst of positive energy and connections among the learners as they leave.

- *Strengthen* the learning community of the group, which is especially important if group members work together or if they have more training days in front of them.

- *Reconnect* learners to each other, to the topic, and to you.
- *Remind* learners of what they have learned.
- *Encourage* learners to make a commitment to use what they've learned.
- *End* the training on an upbeat, positive, and memorable note.

Getting Ready

Materials: Depending upon the activity, learners will need index cards, pens or pencils, noisemakers, and small prizes or training souvenirs—one of each item per person. You will also need a soft throwable object such as a Koosh® or Nerf® ball. Upbeat music is a nice touch, too, so have a music tape or CD and boom box ready. Be sure to familiarize yourself with copyright laws regarding music.

Setup: A special room setup is unnecessary.

Group Size: Any size group is fine.

Ten Celebrations

- **Celebration #1:** *Give a high-five to those in your table group (to the people sitting nearest to you, to all those in your row).* Follow this with a round of applause for all. Note: a high-five is a clap in the air with each learner in a pair using one hand to clap her partner's hand.

- **Celebration #2:** *Tell your table group one thing you enjoyed about working together. Then give each other a high-ten.* Follow this with a round of applause for all. Note: a high-ten is a high-five done with a learner's two hands clapping another learner's two hands in the air.

- **Celebration #3:** Pass out individual noisemakers as training souvenirs. Say one or more of the following: *Sound your noisemaker if you enjoyed the training. Sound the noisemaker if you learned at least six things that you didn't know before. Make noise if you can share what you've learned with other colleagues. Make noise if you can use what you learned. Sound your noisemaker if you had fun today.*

- **Celebration #4:** Use a soft throwable ball and encourage learners to catch, speak, and quickly toss it to someone else. Say: *When the ball is tossed your way, quickly tell us a word or phrase that sums up your feelings about the training, then toss the ball to someone else.* End with a round of applause for all.

- **Celebration #5:** *On a Post-it® note, write a thank-you or compliment for the person on your right. Stick the note on his or her arm.* Then give everyone a round of applause.

- **Celebration #6:** *On an index card, write a phrase of encouragement or a compliment for the person on your left. Hand that person the card and shake his hand.*

- **Celebration #7:** *On the count of three, let's all shout "Good going, group!"* End with a round of applause for all. Choose a phrase to shout out that is relevant to your training and your audience.

- **Celebration #8:** *Stand and find someone to pair up with (standing triads are OK too). Tell this person what the best part of the training was for you. Then give each other a handshake.*

- **Celebration #9:** *Walk around the room and give at least six people a smile, a verbal farewell, and a high-five.* Follow this with a round of applause for all.

- **Celebration #10:** Pass out individual training souvenirs. Say: *Hold up your souvenir. This is to remind you that you make a difference in the lives of those you live and work with. It's also a reminder of what you learned today.* Then end with a round of applause for all.

¡Tips and Variations!

Do It with Them. Deliver the activity instructions with enthusiastic energy, and participate in the activity yourself so that the Celebration feels totally inclusive.

Bow and Smile. If some learners are uncomfortable with hand touches such as handshakes and high-fives, they can simply bow and smile. Let learners know they have that option.

Evaluate, Then Celebrate. If you do have evaluation forms for learners to complete, make sure they know that a Celebration activity will follow. Many training participants think that filling out the evaluation is the last thing they need to do before they leave. When most (not necessarily all) are ready, begin the Celebration.

A Joyful Note. If possible, have upbeat music playing either during or right after the Celebration activity as learners walk out the door. Music also contributes to the boost of positive energy at the end of the training. As previously stated, check with international copyright law (on the Internet) and your company's policy regarding the use of music.

Inside-Outside Circles. If the group is large enough (twenty or more people), learners can form two circles, one facing the other. Then both circles move to the right—because they are facing each other, each circle will be moving in an opposite direction. Everyone gives each person they meet a high-five until they come back to the person they originally faced. Or have them stop the movement after passing a few people. They tell the person they are facing how they plan to use what they learned and what they enjoyed the most about the training. They give this person a handshake.

Do a TENS. Learners stand and do a quick TENS (the letters stand for "Thanks, Eye-contact, Name, Smile") with everyone in the room. They can also shake each person's hand while saying thanks.

Looks Like, Sounds Like. Table groups stand and each group creates a quick sound or motion to represent how they feel about the training. They do their sound or motion to applause.

Standing Ovations. If the training group is small (under twenty), each person quickly stands, bows, and sits while the whole group gives the standing person a round of applause. Or individuals take turns moving to the front of the room, bowing, and then returning to their place, while the whole group gives each person a standing ovation. Give participants the option of passing and remaining seated if they are uncomfortable receiving a standing ovation.

Create Your Own!

Can you think of other Celebration ideas? Write them here.

Take Five!

Five- and Ten-Minute Games That Help Learners RAP It Up: Reinforce, Apply, and Practice

Quick Start

Mark-Up: Circle the activities in the list below that learners could do in five or ten minutes.

Read one article about the training topic.

Stand, stretch, and hold a discussion.

Skim a textbook table of contents.

Create a list of training goals.

Write postcards to themselves.

Ask and answer some questions.

Analyze given data.

Explain the steps in a procedure.

Make a list of facts that they already know about the training topic.

Memorize a number of facts or key concepts.

Debate an important issue.

Express a personal opinion verbally or in writing.

Play a short game.

Walk outside and back while talking to a friend.

Challenge an opinion that differs from others.

Evaluate the pros and cons surrounding an issue.

Demonstrate a procedure.

Of course you circled all the items because you already know a number of quick ways to involve learners in their own learning. The above list is a short example of the wide variety of activities that can help learners reinforce, apply, and practice what they learned. You will add the five- and ten-minute games in this part of the book to what you already know.

Picture This

You are attending a one-hour, in-house customer service workshop with about twenty other employees. As you enter the training room, the facilitator Paul hands you one of two pieces of a postcard. When everyone has arrived, Paul announces, "Stand and find the person who has the other half of the postcard you hold. This person is your postcard partner. Put your postcard together and then discuss the question on the back of the card. You will have about three minutes to do so."

After a minute of comparing postcard fragments, you find your postcard partner, put the card together, and agree on an answer to the card question: "What is the customer service skill that is the most essential to excellent service? Be ready to share your question and answer with the group."

After the three minutes pass, Paul asks for volunteers to share their postcard questions and answers. To make the exercise more interesting, each card had a different question. Others included:

What is the most frequent customer service challenge in our company?

What is our company's greatest customer service strength?

What is one desirable service idea our company hasn't yet implemented?

What is one new customer service strategy our company should consider?

Two minutes of postcard questions and answers follow.

Paul invites everyone to thank their postcard partners and sit down. He verbally summarizes the postcard discussions and points out the connections between the questions and the goals of the workshop. Then he reviews four elements of quality customer service, inviting you and the other employees to add your ideas to the dialogue.

After about ten minutes of lecture, Paul designates one side of the training room as the "strongly agree" side and the other as the "strongly disagree" side. He states a customer service problem that is common in your company and suggests a resolution to the situation. He directs you to stand near the side of the room that designates your agreement or disagreement with his solution. You can also stand in the middle of the room if you want more information or more time to think about it. It takes about a minute for everyone to take a stand. Then Paul leads a three-minute discussion about the situation and the pros and cons of each side. Finally, he asks everyone to signal by raising a hand if this is the response to the problem that the company should take. He thanks the group for their ideas and opinions.

When everyone is seated again, Paul sums up the four customer service elements and how they can be used to deal with the company's service issues. Then he announces that you will play a short game to get a chance to win a prize and to celebrate the learning.

Paul directs you to take an index card and write down a question and answer pertaining to customer service and what you just learned. You give your question a point value: any number between one and ten, with one an easy, yes-no question and ten a difficult question that needs an explanation for an answer.

Paul has you form seated groups of four to five people. He gives each group a plastic toy ear. He spells out the rules of the game: "One person in each group reads his question aloud. The person in the group who grabs the ear first gets a chance to answer the question. If she answers correctly, she gets the point value on the card. If she answers incorrectly, she loses those points or stays at zero. Group members take turns reading their question cards. The reader of each round may not grab the ear. At the end of five minutes, the person with the most points wins the game."

Your group enthusiastically plays the game, with everyone trying to grab the ear during each round. The room fills with friendly competition, laughter, and quiet conversation about the question cards. After five minutes, Paul stops the game, awards toy prizes (plastic ears) to the winners and consolation prizes (small hand clappers) to everyone else. He ends the workshop with, "Now give yourselves a round of applause for your enthusiastic participation in this customer service workshop."

As you walk out the door, you ask Paul the names of the three games he used. He replies, "Postcard Partners, Take a Stand, and Grab That Spoon." Then he smiles and adds, "We really played Grab That Ear instead, because this was a customer service workshop, and I figured that the plastic ear represented listening to a customer, which is a key service skill." You thank him for including such enjoyable and memorable games.

Why Take Five?

In the United States, "Take five!" is a familiar filmmaking phrase that signifies a short rest or break. Ironically, with the longer commercial time between American televised program segments, the phrase could now refer to commercial breaks. As you read in the introduction to *The Ten-Minute Trainer*, after about ten minutes of television viewing, Americans take about a five-minute commercial break.

Although television viewers may grumble about commercial breaks, their bodies are probably loving these break times. Most viewers stand up and move around during commercials—even if it's only to walk to the kitchen or the bathroom. The human body thrives on movement and feels lethargic when it has been sitting too long.

In this book, Take Five! refers to games and activities that learners can do in five or ten minutes. This is long enough for the games to include some movement, as well as review, and short enough that most trainers can fit them in, even with extensive material to cover.

These activities also RAP ("wrap") up the learning, that is, they provide time for learners to reinforce, apply, and practice what they've learned.

What "Take Five!" Games Can Do

With these games, you can reinforce a lot of learning in a little time, especially when you don't have time to play longer games. Five or ten minutes is enough time to include a skills practice or a longer discussion period. With more time to talk about what they learned, participants deepen their conceptual understanding and begin to apply the information to real life. A five- or ten-minute activity also gives learners time to use more higher-order thinking skills such as evaluation and synthesis; that is, they can discuss how to use the material in a variety of ways and how to combine it with other information in new and different ways. In addition to all this, many of these activities include the added bonus of physical movement.

Use these games to open or close a training, before or after a break, or between content segments when you want a longer review activity. Some of the games include a little lighthearted competition, which is always an energy boost for most training participants.

Five or ten minutes of active participation will help learners

- *Repeat and review,* in a variety of fun and interesting ways, what has been learned in the training.
- *Remember* the information for longer periods.
- *Link* what they are learning to what they already know.
- *Increase* both short-term and long-term memory of important information.
- *Remain* alert and involved throughout the training.
- *Keep* their minds involved and their bodies energized.
- *Share* best practices with each other.

- *Challenge* each other with content-related questions.
- *Brainstorm* together, linking additional information to what they just learned.
- *Explore* many ways to make the training content practical and useful in their own lives.
- *Engage* in higher-order thinking skills (examples: categorization, application, judgment, problem solving, evaluation, synthesis), as well as simple memorization of important facts.
- *Practice* a skill related to what they just learned.
- *Coach* each other during the skill practice.
- *Give* each other feedback about the skill being practiced.
- *Apply* what has been learned to real-life situations.
- *Evaluate* the usefulness of what they are learning.
- *Synthesize* old learning with new to create new ways of using what they've learned.

Another Bird's-Eye View of the "Take Five!" Games

So that you don't have to flip back to Chapter One, below is the detailed list again of the five- and ten-minute games:

- *Postcard Partners.* Use this as an opening game to connect learners to each other and to the training topic or concepts.
- *The Gallery Walk.* This can be an opening activity, a review activity, or a closing exercise. Or use it as an ongoing activity throughout the training or during training breaks.
- *Take a Stand.* This is either an opening activity or a review activity when you want participants to discuss topic-related issues.
- *Grab That Spoon.* As a closing exercise, this is a competitive game for a general review. Or include each game round, that is, one question and answer, at various times throughout the training to review specific concepts.
- *Place Your Order.* Use this game to review procedural concepts during the training, that is, information that needs to be learned in a certain order.
- *Metaphor Magic.* This is a creative, right-brain way of reviewing concepts that makes learners think about what they have learned in unique and unusual ways. It can also be a creative closing activity.

- *Let's Trade.* Use this as a closing game in which participants make a commitment to use what they learned.
- *Each One Teach One.* Use this as a kinesthetic exercise to help learners practice skills or review information in an active, hands-on way.
- *The Walkabout.* This is a closing kinesthetic activity that is also high-energy and celebratory.
- *Blackout Bingo.* Use this as another high-energy, closing game. It is also a kinesthetic review exercise.

¡Tips and Variations!

Materials at Hand. For the games that need certain materials, make sure that you have a sufficient number of items for everyone. So that you don't waste valuable training time, pass out the materials before the training, or have them ready and available on the tables or chairs when participants enter the room.

Tell the *Why*. If you feel it is necessary, preface the activities with the *why* behind the *how*. Explain that these short games will actually help participants remember more of the material when the training is over. In addition, you can post the "What 'Take Five!' Games Can Do" list in a visible place in the room and refer to it occasionally as a reminder of what the activity take-aways are.

The Right to Pass. Let participants know that they have the right to pass on any game; that is, they may simply observe if they so choose. This reduces any resistance strong watchers (those who learn more by observation than by doing) may have. It also allows anyone who is tired of interacting to simply take an activity break while still remaining involved in the learning.

From One to Ten. Choose any sixty-second activity and lengthen it to about five or ten minutes by adding processing time at the end of the activity. For example, lead a large-group discussion about what participants learned from the activity. Or answer questions that came up during the activity. Elicit additional information to add to what learners said. Add your own comments and any other information important to the learned material.

Sixty Plus Sixty. Combine a variety of sixty-second activities to create a five-minute opening, review, or closing. For example, do a Quick Start, a Doodle, and a Pair Share, followed by a Shout Out and a Pop-Up.

Here is a specific example of combining these activities: At the opening of a train-the-trainer workshop, participants read the Quick Start, which tells them to draw a cartoon (Doodle) representing what they want to learn. They explain their doodle to the persons sitting next to them (Pair Share). The instructor asks the whole group to state ten things they all want to learn (Shout Out). The instructor tells everyone to form a standing group and share one thing each person already knows about the topic before they sit back down (Pop-Up).

Rehearse the Script. Memorize the game instructions so that you can state them quickly and clearly. Make sure you are clear in your own mind about the activity goals and outcomes related to your training topic.

Explain It. During the training, be sure to include a minute or two to explain the game instructions. This can be part of the activity time or, if time allows, it can precede the activity. Always make sure most of your learners know what to do before beginning the game. To check for understanding, do one of the following:

- Ask a series of yes-and-no questions about the game instructions and have learners signal *yes* with a hand clap and *no* with a foot stomp.
- Have learners tell each other what they think the instructions are; if there is apparent confusion, explain the instructions again.
- Tell learners a true or false statement about the instructions and have them show you thumbs up for true and thumbs down for false.
- Check to see whether they have any questions about the instructions before beginning the game.

Have a Signal. Choose an appropriate signal that will let learners know the game time has ended (a noisemaker, a hand clap, turning the lights off and on, and so forth). Be sure your learners know what the signal is before the game begins. Another option is to assign a Timer for the whole group or, if learners are doing the activity in small groups, direct each group to choose a Timer.

Post Them. Post the game instructions where everyone can see them in case learners need to refer to them as they participate. And remember to keep the instructions simple enough so that learners can do the activity quickly and easily.

Walk and Watch. Walk around and monitor the game, answer questions, and make your own observations that you can later share with the learners.

Discuss It. After the game is over, and if you have a few extra moments, facilitate a whole-group discussion about what participants learned. The discussion may be part of the activity time or may be in addition to it. Just remember that processing an activity deepens the learning in ways that participation alone can't. It's all up to you and the time available.

Wrapping It Up

With "Take Five!" games, learners RAP (wrap) up the learning by reinforcing, applying, and practicing what they learned. These activities help make the learning stick; that is, learners will remember information longer because they've had time to use the information in various ways. These games also save you time that you might have had to spend reteaching the same material later. With these games, the probability increases that participants will use more of what they learned and will remember it longer.

All learning IS experience.
Everything else is just information.
—Albert Einstein

Early to Finish

Mark-Up. Refer to the "What 'Take Five!' Games Can Do" list and underline three items you feel are the most important. Compare these items with the ones you circled in the sixty-second activity introduction. Similarities? Differences? What does this reveal about what you consider important training outcomes?

Reviewing the two lists will also help you remember the activity objectives. Knowing these, you can explain them to your learners, colleagues, and anyone who asks you why you do what you do.

Postcard Partners

What Is a Postcard Partner?

A Postcard Partner is an opening game that connects learners to each other and to the topic in an entertaining way. Each learner chooses a piece of a postcard, then stands and finds his partner or partners—the participants in the group who have the other pieces that go with his postcard. When they find each other, they form standing  pairs or triads, and put their postcard together. They turn the card over and answer a topic-related question or discuss a topic-related issue that is written on the back.

What Does a Postcard Partner Do?

As a connecting activity at the opening of your training, this is one of the best ways to get training participants physically moving while solving a problem— that of finding their postcard partners and then answering a topic-related question. With the Postcard Partner game, learners

- *Connect* with each other and the topic.
- *Begin* to form a learning community for the duration of the training.
- *Focus* on the topic, what they already know, questions to answer, or issues to discuss.
- *Begin* a dialogue about the training concepts.
- *Move* physically around the room, thus raising the energy level of the group.

 # Getting Ready

Materials: Before the training begins, purchase (or make) a set of postcards with a picture on the front. Although different postcard pictures make the activity more interesting, you can also use colored index cards. You will need enough postcards for one-half the group size (if you cut the cards into halves) or one-third the group size (if you cut the cards into thirds). Print a sentence on the back of each card. The sentences can be the same or different for each postcard. They can be topic-related questions to answer or issues to discuss. Examples are:

- What are three facts you already know about the training topic?
- What is a question you want answered today concerning this topic?
- What are two things you want to be able to do as a result of this training?
- Here is an issue related to this topic (state the issue). What is your opinion about this?
- Discuss this statement (make a statement about the topic).
- What is an issue that you feel is crucial to this topic?

Cut each card a different way—diagonals, zigzags, waves, straight, curved—so that it is easier for partners to find each other. Put the mixed-up card pieces into a small bag or box. If you aren't sure how many participants will be in the training, estimate the number and then make a few extra cards just in case. Participants can always share a piece, too.

Setup: The room must be large enough to accommodate movement with enough space between tables, chairs, and walls for people to walk as they hunt for their partners.

Group Size: The group size can be small (at least six people) or large (up to thirty). As the group size gets bigger, it takes more time for learners to find their partners and more time to process the questions and statements. It also takes more time for you to make the postcards.

Time: Ten minutes. To do a five-minute version, skip the processing step (see the activity instructions) or include it later in the training in the form of a sixty-second Shout Out. If the group is small enough (under a dozen), direct learners to introduce their partners to the whole group before they summarize their postcard discussions.

Postcard Partner Instructions

- Place a small bag or box filled with postcard pieces by the door. Tell participants to take a piece from the bag or box as they enter the training room. If you have table groups, place the postcard pieces on the tables. If anyone ends up without a piece or a partner, have that person join one of the other postcard groups.

- Tell participants to find their postcard partner(s) by moving around the room and checking postcards until they find the ones that complete the pieces they are holding. This will take about a minute or two, depending upon the size of the group.

- When participants have found their postcard partners, they put the card pieces together and then turn the card over. Give them about three minutes to discuss the question or statement on the back.

- Process the activity by having partners report out to the whole group. They can read the card questions or statements and then verbally respond. Or they can simply summarize what they discussed. If the group is large, ask for a few volunteers to report to the whole group—not every pair or triad needs to report. This will take about four to five minutes.

- Postcard partners thank each other and give each other a round of applause. Then they return to their seats.

¡Tips and Variations!

Regional or Thematic Postcards. Use postcards that picture the location the training is in (town, city, region, state). Or use cards related to a training concept.

Homemade Postcards. Make up your own postcards using blank index cards, large stick-on labels, and graphics from computer clip art or from digital photos. If your training has an overall theme, make the postcards theme-related. You can also glue magazine pictures onto index cards or construction paper.

Learner-Created Postcards. Working in pairs, learners can also make and cut their own postcards. They put the pieces in a bag or box and mix them up. Then each learner draws out a piece and takes part in the activity.

Postcards to Review or Celebrate. Learners can also do the activity as a review in the middle of a training or as a celebration for the closing.

Connect Again. If the training is lengthy, have learners reconnect with the same postcard partners later in the day to review and discuss what they are learning.

Create Your Own!

Add your own Postcard Partner ideas to this box.

The Gallery Walk

What Is a Gallery Walk?

The Gallery Walk is a powerful opening, closing, or review activity. In this activity, participants write on various pieces of chart paper that you've taped to the training room walls. With the Gallery Walk, you can gather a lot of learner-created information in a little time. The activity is easily adaptable to the training goals, your learners' needs, the size of the group, and the learning environment.

You create the chart pages before the training. The chart pages may contain topic-related questions to answer, sentences to finish, or concepts to learn. First, learners walk from chart to chart, writing their responses to the different items on the charts. Then they take a "gallery walk," touring the room, reading the charts, and observing patterns, surprises, or anything interesting on the charts that they would like to comment about later.

What Does a Gallery Walk Do?

Depending upon your purpose in using this activity, a Gallery Walk can

- *Connect* learners to both new and old information.
- *Help* learners focus on what they already know and what they want to learn.
- *Build* a strong learning community by connecting learners to each other and to the topic.
- *Gather* a large amount of topic-related information to be used later in the training.
- *Be* a pre- and post-training self-assessment for learners.
- *Act* as a needs-assessment for you so that you can make sure participants' learning needs are being addressed during the training.
- *Provide* learners with an opportunity to physically move around while reviewing material.

- *Encourage* learners to use higher-order thinking skills (example: analysis, evaluation, synthesis) while engaged in a review.

- *Provide* time for learners to respond to topic-related issues that they might not otherwise have had the time to address.

- *Allow* learners to be completely honest because their written responses are anonymous.

- *Give* learners the opportunity to make written commitments to use the new information.

- *Become* a thoughtful, high-energy way to either open or close a training.

 # Getting Ready

Materials: Before the training, create topic-related questions, sentences to complete, or concepts, one per chart paper, and print them in large dark lettering so that they are readable from at least four to six feet away. Some examples for an opening Gallery Walk are:

- One fact I already know about this topic
- One take-away I want from this training
- One question I want answered
- How I plan to use what I learn
- One thing I know about (state a training concept)
- My strength (related to this topic)
- An issue or challenge (related to this topic)
- Topic trivia

For a review or a closing, chart items might include:

- What are some problems related to these concepts?
- How would you address this issue (state a topic-related issue)?
- What is a creative way you could use this information in your own work?
- How does this concept link with what you already know?
- List ways you can apply what you're learning.

- List facts you can add to what you've already learned.
- What is a question you still have about this information?

The number of chart papers should equal approximately one for every four to six participants. This way, whether learners work individually or in groups, there are a sufficient number of charts for most of them to be writing at one time. Learners will need broad-tipped felt pens of dark colors (regular ballpoint pens or pencils can't be read from afar)—one per participant or per writing group. If you play music during the activity, you will need music tapes or CDs and a boom box or sound system.

Setup: There needs to be enough wall space to hang charts and enough space in the room for participants to walk around without bumping into furniture. If there is not enough physical space or wall space to accommodate the activity, read the Tips and Variations for other ways to do a Gallery Walk.

Group Size: The group should be more than ten but fewer than fifty. The activity can be done with groups larger than fifty, but doing so takes more preparation and participation time, not to mention more wall and room space. The optimal group size is around thirty.

Time: Ten minutes. To do a five-minute version, do only the writing and reading steps of the Gallery Walk, saving the discussion and processing steps for another five-minute break later in the training. Or do only the writing step, then later the reading step, and finally the processing step, thereby making the activity an ongoing part of the training. See the activity instructions for descriptions of these steps.

Gallery Walk Instructions

- Announce the purpose for the activity. Tell learners they will work either individually or cooperatively (depending upon how you want them to work). Direct them to move from chart to chart, writing their responses on the charts. If they finish before time is called, they can begin reading the charts. Give the whole group about three minutes to write on as many charts as they can. Play upbeat music during this time.
- When the writing time is over, tell learners to take a walk around the gallery, reading the charts and observing any interesting patterns, surprising comments, unusual responses, and so forth. They will report their observations to their table groups or the people who were seated near them before the activity

began. Allow another two minutes to do this part of the activity. Play slower music during this time.

• Tell learners to return to their table groups or seats and discuss their observations (about three minutes). Process this discussion by having each table group give a summary of its discussion. Or ask volunteers to share their observations. Allow at least two minutes or more for the processing time. Summarize the processing with your own observations and tie the summary to the activity purpose.

¡Tips and Variations!

Gallery Walk Breaks. For a full-day training, divide up the writing portion of the activity into short stretch breaks throughout the morning. Give learners enough time to stand, stretch, write on one chart, and sit. They can do the rest of the activity (chart reading, discussion, and processing) in the afternoon.

More Gallery Walk Breaks. Learners do the writing and reading parts of the activity at standard break times (morning, lunch, and afternoon). Then they do the discussion and processing together as part of the review or closing activities.

Pass the Charts. If space to move around the room is limited, instead of posting the chart papers on walls, put one at each table and have table groups write responses and then pass the papers to other groups.

Table Rotation. Put charts on tables and have table groups stand and rotate from table to table as they write.

Card Charts. Instead of writing on the wall charts, have participants write their answers on large index cards or Post-it® notes and tape them to the charts.

Graffiti Gallery. Cover one entire wall with chart or butcher paper and label it the Graffiti Gallery. At designated times during the training, participants write their responses to a question you ask or to a topic-related problem. They can also write their opinions about a concept, a question they have, a comment they want to share, and so forth.

Create Your Own!

Write more Gallery Walk variations in the box below.

Take a Stand

What Is Take a Stand?

In traditional training sessions, learners remain seated while participating in small group discussions about topic-related issues. With Take a Stand, learners move around the room and choose a designated place to stand before engaging in small group discussions. In effect, the activity includes kinesthetic (movement) and spatial (visual) ways of learning as well as linguistic (verbal).

Take a Stand also encourages learners to use higher-order thinking skills (analysis, evaluation, synthesis) as they discuss their own perceptions and opinions of questions, issues, or concepts related to what they are learning.

During the activity, one side of the training room represents one topic-related issue, problem, statement, or viewpoint, and the other side represents the opposite (the sides can also represent "strongly agree" versus "strongly disagree," with the middle of the room representing "undecided or need more information"). Participants stand and move to one side or the other (or any place in between) to represent their own opinions, feelings, or choices about the issue. They discuss their choices with those around them. Participants on each side can also take turns commenting about their choices in a whole group discussion.

What Does Take a Stand Do?

Take a Stand can be as intense, rich, and thought provoking as time and the topic allow. With this activity, learners can

- *Recognize* important, topic-related concepts and issues.
- *Analyze* their own perceptions of these concepts and issues.
- *Take* an instant position on a topic-related issue.
- *Refine* their own opinions based on the small group discussions about the concepts and issues.

- *Evaluate* the perceptions and opinions of others and whether these will be useful to know.
- *Synthesize* what they've discussed into new ways of perceiving, thinking, and acting.
- *Use* both kinesthetic (movement) and spatial (visual) learning to increase retention.

 # Getting Ready

Materials: Instead of just explaining what each side of the room represents, you may also want to give learners that information in written form. If so, you will need wall charts, overhead transparencies, or computer slides.

Setup: Make sure there is enough space in the room for participants to move to one side of the room or the other or in the middle (for example, large aisles and empty side areas). A large breakout area in the back of the room or hallway would also suffice.

Group Size: To make the activity worth the time, the minimum size group should be about a dozen. There is no maximum limit.

Time: Five minutes. With only five minutes, do one Take a Stand, with one statement or issue. Keep the processing time at the end fairly short (a sixty-second Shout Out works fine). For the ten-minute version, you can fit in two or three rounds of Take a Stand, with more than one issue or statement. Learners move quickly for each statement and discuss each choice with a sixty-second Pair Share. You lead a short, whole group discussion at the end of the Take a Stand rounds.

Take a Stand Instructions

- Explain to the participants what each side of the room represents. Examples are: strongly agree, strongly disagree (for topic-related opinion statements); lots of experience, a little experience (for job-related statements such as use of technology or specific job skills); resident experts, experts in training (for experienced employees and new hires); yes, no (for simple questions). The middle of the room can represent "undecided," "need more information," or "middle of the road."

- Tell learners that they are going to stand and move to either side or any place in between to the spot that most represents their perception or opinion about the stated issue or answer to your stated question. Then tell them the issue, question, or statement. For example, in a customer service training an issue might be: What is the appropriate way to handle a customer service complaint? A question might be: Does this situation constitute poor customer service (name the situation)? A statement might be: The best way to handle poor customer service is to fire the employee who is responsible.
- Once all learners are standing in their chosen places, instruct them to form small standing groups and discuss why they chose to stand in this particular spot. They can also share their own perceptions and opinions of the choices they made.
- Process the whole activity by asking for comments from both sides and from those standing in the middle. You can also process the activity by alternating sides (first a comment from one side, then from the other, and so forth).
- If time allows, have standing groups reform into mixed small groups, with each side represented within each group. Have the mixed groups continue the discussion for a few minutes longer.
- When learners return to their seats, they (or you) can summarize some of the important points from the small and large group discussions. Or they can take a minute or two to do a Think and Write about what they learned from the activity.

¡Tips and Variations!

On a Scale of One to Ten. The space between each side of the room can be a continuum from one extreme to another. For example: one side stands for the number one (I don't know anything about this topic) and the other side for the number ten (I know everything there is to know about this topic). Participants can stand anywhere on this continuum from one to ten.

Four Corners. Instead of using the room's two sides to represent topic-related statements, you can use the room's four corners. For example, the corners stand for strongly agree, strongly disagree, moderately agree, moderately disagree. The middle is "haven't decided yet." Or the corners stand for four jobs, four levels of experience, four issues ("Stand by the most important one"), or four concepts to learn more about ("Stand by the one that interests you the most").

Take the Pulse. To check how the learners are feeling about an issue, ask them to stand on the side of the room that best represents their feelings: strong feelings about this issue versus no feelings about this issue. Or to check how they are feeling about the training, the sides could represent: "All is well—carry on" versus "Stop and talk—I have some concerns."

Create Your Own!

Can you think of more Take a Stand variations? Write them here.

Grab That Spoon!

What Is Grab That Spoon?

Grab That Spoon is a quick review game with a dash of friendly competition. Learners sit in small groups and take turns asking each other questions for points or tokens. The person who first grabs a plastic spoon gets to answer the question. The competition heats up as learners realize that the fastest person has the most chance of winning.

What Does Grab That Spoon Do?

Grab That Spoon is a high-energy way to

- *Review* material quickly and easily.
- *Add* friendly competition to the review.
- *Allow* learners to generate the review questions.
- *Include* physical action in a seated learning activity.
- *Give* learners time to discuss their own understanding of the training concepts.
- *Take* a topic-related, competitive break from the lecture.

 Getting Ready

Materials: Learners will need pens or pencils and index cards (one of each item per person) and plastic spoons (one for each group of four to six people). If you wish to award small prizes for the winners, have enough for one per each group of four to six people. You can also give out small consolation prizes to the nonwinners.

Setup: Learners need to sit at tables in groups of four to six people or in chairs clustered into groups. The plastic spoon for each group must be within reach of all learners (on the table top or, if there are no tables, on an empty chair, the floor, or on a binder balanced on someone's knee).

Group Size: The small groups should have from four to six people. It doesn't matter how many small groups there are.

Time: Five minutes. For the ten-minute version, direct learners to make more than one question-answer card so that they will have a sufficient number of game rounds to play.

Grab That Spoon Instructions

- Each learner writes a review question and answer on an index card. He also writes a point value for the question on the card. Example: points can be from 1–10. A 1-point question is easy to answer with a simple yes/no; a 10-point question is hard to answer with a more lengthy explanation. Another example: easy question = 1 point; moderately hard question = 2 points; challenging question = 3 points.
- One spoon is placed where each learner in the group can reach it (in the middle of the table or, if there are no tables, on a binder or the floor in the middle of the group).
- One person volunteers to be the first reader. This person may not grab the spoon. The reader reads aloud her question. The first group member to grab the spoon answers the question. If correct, the person who answers gets the points. If incorrect, this person loses points or stays at zero points. Group members take turns being the reader and reading their question cards.
- When the time is up, each person adds up his points. The person with the most points in each small group wins applause and high-fives from the group. Or give out small prizes for the winners and consolation prizes for the others.

i Tips and Variations *!*

Grab That Anything. The object doesn't have to be a spoon! Play the game with an object related to the training—something easy to grab that also has to do with the training topic or theme. Examples: "Grab That Mouse" for a computer class, "Grab That Ear" with plastic ears for a communication course, "Grab That Key" for keys to customer service, "Grab That Number" with dice for financial training, "Grab

That Whistle" for safety training. You can use items found in your home or office. You can also purchase small, inexpensive, training-related items from Trainers Warehouse at www.trainerswarehouse.com, Kipp Brothers at www.kippbro.com, or Oriental Trading Company at www.orientaltrading.com. Get their free catalogs and spend a few minutes looking for possible game items and token prizes.

Entire Training Review. Give each learner from two to four index cards. At different times during the training, have learners write on each card a new question-answer pertaining to what they just learned. Then, as an overall review, allow about ten minutes near the end of the training to play the game.

Break-Time Rounds. Play one round (one question asked and answered) at a time, and space rounds throughout the training to make the activity a short, high-energy, ongoing break from the lecture.

Chips, Tokens, or Cards. Instead of points, learners can play for chips or other small tokens. Each group gets a small pile of chips or tokens to use for the game. Or learners can play for a card from a standard card deck. At the end of the activity, the person in the small group, or in the room, with the best poker hand wins.

Trainer-Created Questions. Make up your own review questions and print them on index cards, one set per game group. Have each group play the game using your questions and answers.

Processing Time. If you have time and choose to discuss the activity afterwards, ask open-ended questions such as:

- What was the most important thing you learned from the game?
- What was a question that your group discussed or debated?
- Was there a question with more than one right answer?
- What is a question you still have after playing the game?

Create Your Own!

Write other Grab That Spoon variations in this box.

Place Your Order

What Is Place Your Order?

Place Your Order is a review game in which participants work together to put a series of cards in the correct order. Each card describes a specific step in a topic-related procedure. You provide the card sets and the answer-key cards. Each small group self-corrects by checking its completed card set against the answer key.

The game can be cooperative, with the focus on small group discussion and agreement as to the order of the cards. Or you can make it competitive by assigning a time limit during which groups need to complete the game correctly in order to win prizes.

Place Your Order can also be learner created, whereby small groups create the cards and answer keys, then exchange game sets with other small groups.

Here are a few examples of the kind of procedural steps you can write on the cards: for a beginning computer class, the steps to boot up the computer or run a program; for an accounting course, the steps in reconciling a bank account; for a customer service training, the procedure used in solving a service problem; for a safety workshop, the procedure used in filing a written safety report; for a leadership seminar, the procedure for forming effective work teams; for a first-aid class, the steps in doing the Heimlich procedure; for a training program, the steps in designing an effective lesson or presentation.

What Does Place Your Order Do?

This game gives learners an opportunity to

- *Review* the sequence of steps for topic-related procedures.
- *Analyze* the out-of-order sequence with the goal of putting it in order.
- *Work* cooperatively together toward a common goal.

- *Evaluate* information and make decisions based on the evaluations.
- *Decide* whether they agree with what other learners perceive as the correct order.
- *Discuss* differences of perceptions and opinions.
- *Apply* what they have learned to specific, job-related situations.

 Getting Ready

Materials: Make a sufficient number of card sets and answer keys for all small groups. Or if the game is learner created, each small group will need a stack of index cards and pens or pencils. If the game is competitive, have ample small prizes for the winners and consolation prizes for everyone else. You may wish to post the game instructions where everyone can see them.

Setup: Learners should sit in table groups of four to six people or in clustered groups of chairs. The group materials must be within reach of all learners (on the table top or, if there are no tables, on an empty chair or on the floor).

Group Size: The small groups should have from four to six people in them. It doesn't matter how many small groups there are.

Time: Five minutes. For the ten-minute version, have small groups make the card sets during one five-minute training segment (example: before lunch), and then play the game during another five-minute segment (after lunch). Or for a two-day training, game making is a homework assignment. Then learners play the games on day two.

Place Your Order Instructions

- Explain the game purpose and instructions to the whole group. Pass out card sets and answer keys to each small group. Or if learners are going to create the card sets and answer keys, make sure that each small group has ample index cards and pens or pencils to do so.
- Tell the learners to work together within their small groups to put the cards in order. When finished, they check their answers against the answer key. If you make the game competitive, inform learners as to the time limit in which to

correctly complete the task. More than one table group can win if they do it correctly before the time is up.

- If you decide that participants will create the game cards and answer keys, assign different procedures to each small group. Some procedures can be the same, but there should be enough variety so that not all tables are reviewing and printing the same steps. For example, in a job-search class, one group might write the steps for an Internet job-search procedure, another for résumé writing, another for a job interview, and another for job accreditation procedures. Each small group makes its step-by-step procedure cards, one step printed on each card. Each group also creates a card with an answer key. Small groups mix up their cards and pass them, along with the answer key face down, to other groups. Then group members work together to put the new set of cards in order.

- Signal learners when time is up, have them check their answers, and give their group a round of applause if they placed the cards in the correct order. If time allows and groups have card sets describing different procedures, they can exchange card sets again and play another round.

¡Tips and Variations!

What's Missing? With a learner-created game, direct each table group to leave out one or two procedural steps as the group prints the steps on the cards. On the answer key, the groups list all steps, including the ones left out. The table group receiving the card set has to put them in order and fill in the missing steps by printing these on blank index cards and inserting them where they belong in the sequence.

Myth or Fact? Instead of a Place Your Order card game, groups play a Myth or Fact card game. Table groups print a number of myths and facts that are topic related—one myth or fact per index card. On the back of the card, they print the answer "Myth" or "Fact" and a point value for each card. They mix up the cards and pass them, face up, to another group. The second group discusses each card and places the myth cards in one pile and the fact cards in another. They check their answers by turning over the cards. They add up their correct points and give themselves a cheer if they got them all.

Match-Up. Instead of Place Your Order cards, groups create Match-Up cards. Group members work together to choose and print important training terms on one set of cards and the matching definitions on another card set. Groups also create answer keys with point values. Groups exchange cards and match terms with definitions for the points.

Mix 'Em Up. Assign a different type of card game for each small group to make. For example, one group makes a Place Your Order game. Another makes a Match-Up game. A third group makes a Myth or Fact game. When table groups exchange card games, each plays a different game. If time allows, groups exchange games again for another round. If playing competitively, groups keep track of each game's points and applaud the group with the most points after the game's end.

Trainer-Made Games. Premake a variety of different card games (Place Your Order, Myth or Fact, Match-Up) with enough copies for each small group to play at one time. Use small boxes or manila envelopes to hold the game cards and answer keys. Table groups exchange games during a designated review time. Or put all game envelopes on a "Game Table" and have each group choose a game to play at different times during the training. You can also combine ready-made games with learner-created games.

Ongoing Games. Table groups create games during an early training segment, play one round during the middle of the training, play a second round later, and finish with a third round as part of the closing activities.

Create Your Own!

Brainstorm more Place Your Order or other card games here.

Metaphor Magic!

What Is Metaphor Magic?

This activity uses the power of metaphors and analogies to capture the essence of a training concept. Metaphors and analogies are phrases that compare one thing with another thing that is unlike the first. Metaphors are right-brain training tools because they create mental images that instantly communicate concepts, without the need for long explanations.

For example, sometimes we trainers feel as though we are going against the grain, trudging uphill, spoon-feeding our learners, with the odds stacked against us. Other times we feel as though we are a beacon in the night, making headway, going with the flow, capturing the hearts of our learners, and turning them on to learning. All these phrases are metaphors, strung together to show you that most cultures embed metaphors into everyday language.

Colorful phrases, sayings, comparisons, idioms, and the like are all metaphors. Each language has its own vivid metaphors that people use in their everyday lives. Why? *Because metaphors save time.* A mental picture can get the point across much more quickly than a lengthy explanation can. For example, consider these American metaphors:

- It's raining cats and dogs.
- She's one brick shy of a full load.
- He thinks he's the cat's meow.
- It's on the tip of my tongue.
- She's burning the candle at both ends.
- It happens once in a blue moon.
- He's blind as a bat.
- It hit me like a bolt out of the blue.

If American English is your mother tongue, you instantly understand the messages behind the metaphors. If you're from another culture, you most probably can understand the context of the metaphors, especially if they are part of a sentence ("She makes so many mistakes that I think she's one brick shy of a full load." Or, "I was trying to think of what to say and then it hit me like a bolt out of the blue."). Here are the meanings of these American metaphors:

- It's raining cats and dogs. *It's raining very hard.*
- She's one brick shy of a full load. *She lacks intelligence.*
- He thinks he's the cat's meow. *He thinks very highly of himself.*
- It's on the tip of my tongue. *I almost remember it.*
- She's burning the candle at both ends. *She's working too hard.*
- It happens once in a blue moon. *It happens only occasionally.*
- He's blind as a bat. *He's really shortsighted.*
- It hit me like a bolt out of the blue. *Suddenly I understood.*

In terms of training, you don't have to use culturally biased metaphors. Ordinary household objects, things found in nature, items in a wallet or handbag—any everyday thing or experience can become a metaphor for a training concept.

What Does Metaphor Magic Do?

When you use metaphors, you create mental images that stick in a learner's mind. The image is an almost instantaneous understanding of something that might take paragraphs to explain otherwise. Training without using metaphors is like traveling by car—driving from point A through points B, C, D, and so on to reach point Z. Using metaphors while training is like traveling by plane—from point A to point Z without having to waste time going through all the other points along the way. This is an example of using a metaphor to explain a concept.

A note for language experts: You know the differences between metaphors and analogies, or metaphors and similes. But for the sake of this book and the Metaphor Magic activity, we will refer to them all as variations of the same right-brain training method, that is, using comparisons and vivid mental imagery to deepen the learners' conceptual understanding of what you are teaching.

With metaphors, learners can

- *Link* new learning to vivid mental images.
- *Increase* long-term memory of important concepts.
- *Think* and remember in creative, unique ways.
- *Understand* the essence of a concept more quickly and more deeply.
- *Make* complicated concepts simple to grasp.
- *Use* higher-order thinking skills (analysis, evaluation, synthesis).
- *Learn* faster and remember more.

 # Getting Ready

Materials: You will need a chart tablet and stand (or overhead projector and transparencies—anything you can write on that all learners will be able to see), broad-tipped colored felt pens (at least two, in dark colors), one chart paper posted where everyone can see it and titled: "[Training concept] is like a [household object] because. . . ." Depending upon the metaphor strategy you choose, learners may need some of the following items: one small bag or box per table group containing small household objects or toys, a half-dozen larger household objects, blank chart paper or overhead transparencies (one sheet of each per table group), colorful broad-tipped felt pens or transparency pens (three or four per table group).

Setup: Place the chart stand and tablet where everyone can see them. Ask for a volunteer to write on the chart for you. Learners should be seated in small table groups so that they can work together. Learners may also need physical space in which to move around.

Group Size: Any size group is fine.

Time: Five minutes. For the ten-minute version, increase the number of metaphors each small group needs to create. Or do one of the variations. Another option is to increase the processing time, making sure that all groups get a chance to share their metaphors.

Metaphor Magic Instructions

- Ask the whole group to state the names of five to six household objects from any room, including the garage. Print these in list format down one side of a chart paper or overhead transparency. Then direct the whole group to state five to six training concepts they've learned. Print this list down the other side of the chart or transparency. Post the chart paper or transparency where it is visible to everyone.

- Direct learners' attention to the chart paper on which is printed: "[Training concept] is like a [household object] because. . . ." Tell learners to work in small groups to finish the sentence, using both lists of objects and training concepts. Direct them to create three metaphors using one concept and one object from the lists. They can print their ideas on chart paper or simply be ready to report their metaphors to the whole group. Give them about three minutes to make up their sentences. Some examples:

> Customer service is like a broom because you sweep problems away, you clean up messes that other people make, and some of your customers are witches!

> Training is like a food blender because you throw in lots of ingredients (people, information, activities), you mix them up, and you end up with a delicious learning experience.

> A financial planning program is like a car engine because when it's running smoothly it carries you to your future goals, and when it breaks down it costs you a lot to get it in good running order again.

- Ask for volunteers to report a few of their metaphors to the whole group. Applaud those who do so.

¡Tips and Variations!

Object Display. Instead of simply listing the household objects, bring in a number of objects, put them on display in the front of the room, and have small groups do the Metaphor Magic activity by using these objects.

It's in the Bag. Place a lunch bag filled with three to five small, household objects or toys on each table. Direct table groups to choose an object from the bags and then do the activity using that object. Small objects can include paper clips, staplers, erasers, eating utensils, drinking cups, paper napkins, scissors, hammers, nails, hand towels, razors, stuffed animals, race cars, plastic statues, shoes, soap, matches, jewelry, photos, tweezers, and so forth. Be creative. Put different objects in each bag.

How Does It Look? Have each small group make up its own visual metaphor by drawing it on chart paper and explaining it to the whole group. For visual metaphors, groups can use items in nature, experiences, stories, movie titles, famous people (living or dead), as well as objects. For example, in a team-building training, a group might draw a tree and explain that the company is the tree trunk, the team-building skills are the branches (they label the branches with the specific skills they've learned), and the branches hold the leaves (team members) together.

Make It 3-D. Set up a table with craft materials on it. These can include Play-Doh®, pipe cleaners, feathers, colored paper, clay, felt squares, ribbon, crepe paper, balloons, stickers, wooden sticks, toys, Legos™, art materials, and so forth. Working in small groups, learners use the craft materials to create 3-D representations of training concepts. Give them about five minutes to create their metaphoric sculptures and about thirty seconds per group to explain their creations to the whole group. Follow each explanation with applause.

How Does It Sound? Working in small groups, learners create a sound or movement to represent a training concept. They present their sound or movement to the whole group. Follow each presentation with applause. Learners can also use noisemakers or musical instruments as sounds to represent concepts.

Create Your Own!

Let your creativity shine with your own Metaphor Magic variations.

Let's Trade

What Is Let's Trade?

In Let's Trade, learners write a comment, question, or piece of information, as directed by you, on an index card. Then learners walk around the room, trading cards a number of times. At the end of the activity, they do something with the card, as per your instructions. For example, they can read the cards aloud, ask or answer the questions aloud, create a short demonstration to teach the card's concept, or discuss the cards that they consider the most important.

Participants will often share a comment or question anonymously that they wouldn't otherwise share in front of the whole group. Let's Trade allows learners to remain anonymous even as they participate in the activity itself.

You can find an excellent variation of this activity, called the Values Envelopes Game, in Sivasailam (Thiagi) Thiagarajan's *Design Your Own Games and Activities* (2003, p. 13).

What Does Let's Trade Do?

With this activity, learners can

- *Write* comments, questions, or concerns anonymously without fear of sounding "stupid."
- *Analyze* and rank order important training concepts or learner-created questions.
- *Review* what the whole group considers to be the most important information.
- *Discuss* learner-created questions and issues.
- *Demonstrate* their understanding of the training concepts.
- *Move* around the room while reviewing, questioning, and discussing.

 Getting Ready

Materials: Learners will need index cards and pens or pencils—one item per person.

Setup: There needs to be enough space between furniture and around the perimeter of the room so that participants can stand and walk.

Group Size: At least a dozen or more participants are needed to make the activity work well. There is no upper limit to the group size.

Time: Five minutes. For the ten-minute version, choose one of the variations, do more trading rounds, or extend the processing time.

Let's Trade Instructions

• Tell participants to print a topic-related question on an index card. Then each person stands and trades his card with someone who is standing near him. After the first trade, learners walk around the room and trade cards again until they have traded at least two more times. They cannot take their own cards back.

• Tell participants to stop trading and read their cards silently. Ask those who have a question they feel is of benefit to the whole group to read their cards aloud, one at a time. Give the whole group a minute to respond to each question. Include your own answer, too.

• Discuss as many questions as the five to ten minutes allow. When the time is up, collect the cards. If you have time later, address the rest of the questions. Or post them on a wall chart and invite participants to write their answers on the cards or on the chart.

¡Tips and Variations!

Rank Order the Questions. The best variation of all is to do what Thiagi does in his Values Envelopes Game, mentioned earlier, and rank order the cards. After the first trade, learners pair up with someone who does not have their original card. They assign point values to the two question cards they are holding, dividing ten points between the cards, depending upon the importance of the question. For example, they may decide that one card gets all ten points and the other gets zero points. Or they may give one question three points and the other seven points. They write the points on each card and then trade cards with two other people. Again, they pair up with different partners and assign points to the new cards. They do this one more time. After the trades are over, learners total the points on the cards they hold. The questions with the most totaled points are the ones that participants discuss.

Rank Order the Concepts. Use the variation above, only instead of writing questions on the cards, learners write the most important (to them) training concepts. After participants trade cards and tally the points, they state the three to five top concepts. If time allows, they can state all the concepts in order of the most to least important.

Rank Order the Issues. Do the same as above, only with topic-related issues. After the trading is over, address the top-ranked issues first with a whole group discussion.

Concept Demonstration. If the training concepts are the kind that can be demonstrated (for example, procedural steps in technical training, communication skills, or a customer service procedure), tell participants to demonstrate the concept written on the card they hold. Learners can also form standing groups after the last trade, choose one of their cards, and together with their group members demonstrate that skill.

Action Plans. On one side of the card, learners print their action plans. On the other side, they print their contact information (name, work phone, or e-mail address). They stand and do three trades, making sure that they don't get their own cards back. After the third trade, they keep the cards they have and sit down. Tell learners to write on the card a certain date within a week (or two weeks) from the present. On this date they will contact the person whose card they hold and ask that person how the action plan is coming along. Remind them to keep the card in a visible yet safe place until the contact date.

Create Your Own!

Write more Let's Trade ideas in the box below.

Each One Teach One

What Is Each One Teach One?

This activity gives learners the opportunity to teach and coach each other. Learners pair up and teach each other what they just learned, give each other feedback, practice a skill together, coach each other as they practice, and provide mutual support by encouraging each other. The best way for a learner to reinforce, apply, and practice any new skill is to teach it to someone else. In his book *Illusions*, Richard Bach tells us: "We master what we teach." When participants teach each other, they begin to master the material.

What Does Each One Teach One Do?

With Each One Teach One, expect to see learners

- *Demonstrate* a new skill.
- *Give* each other feedback about how well they are modeling the skill.
- *Coach* each other as they practice the new skill.
- *Discuss* what they learned.
- *Ask* each other questions.
- *Encourage* each other.
- *Provide* mutual support for ongoing learning.

 Getting Ready

Materials: If the new information or new skills require materials (for example, software or computers, or physical tools), have these ready for learners to use during this activity.

Setup: Learners will also need physical space in which to move around if necessary.

Group Size: Any size group is fine, as long as there is enough physical space for participants to practice the skill.

Time: Five minutes. For the ten-minute version, extend the practice time or the processing time.

Each One Teach One Instructions

- Tell participants they will have an opportunity to practice a skill or teach each other what they just learned in the training. Direct them to form standing pairs. If there is an odd number of participants, one pair can become a triad.
- One person in the pair is the learner. The other person is the coach. The learner demonstrates the new skill while explaining it to the coach. The coach gives the learner positive feedback, encouragement, and any help that she may need.
- The partners change roles. They practice the demonstration-coaching session again. If there is no skill to practice, pairs can take turns teaching each other training concepts, explaining the concepts in their own words or discussing ways to use the information in real-life situations. End the activity with partners giving each other a round of applause.
- Process the activity with a few quick questions for the whole group:

What was the most important thing you learned?

How did you feel about your skills?

What was helpful about having a coach?

What other questions came up during the activity?

i Tips and Variations *!*

Teacher and Student. One person becomes the teacher and the other the student. The teacher explains the new information to the student and the student asks the teacher questions about the material. Then they reverse roles and practice again.

Daring Demos. Pairs spend about five minutes creating a thirty- to sixty-second skills demonstration. If time allows, each pair presents its demo to the whole group. If time is short, ask for two or three volunteer pairs to do their demonstrations.

Wrong Way. One person demonstrates the skill, doing a part or step incorrectly. Then he asks, "What's wrong with this?" and his partner answers the question.

Create Your Own!

Are there other variations to Each One Teach One?

The Walkabout

What Is a Walkabout?

Based loosely on the idea of an ancient aboriginal walkabout in the Australian desert, a Walkabout is simply a way to give learners the opportunity to walk and talk at the same time. Instead of sitting or standing in one place, participants form Walkabout pairs or triads, and walk around the room or outside and back in, while reviewing the training material.

Walking, talking, fresh air, exercise—all these can be part of a learning experience. The Walkabout is one way to bring the outdoors into your training—and to keep yourself and your learners awake, alert, and happy all the while.

Besides being a review activity, the Walkabout is also a great, high-energy closing activity.

What Does a Walkabout Do?

By participating in a Walkabout, learners can

- *Take* a topic-related break that includes exercise plus a review of material already learned.
- *Ask* topic-related questions of each other as they walk.
- *Get* some fresh air and exercise while reviewing course material.
- *Make* action plans (how they plan to use the material learned) and share them with each other as part of a closing activity.
- *Discuss* best practices and learn from each other as they walk and talk.
- *Stay* interested, motivated, and awake during long training sessions.

Getting Ready

Materials: Special materials are unnecessary for this activity, unless you want training participants to write Walkabout Reflections (see Tips and Variations) afterwards. If so, learners will need writing materials.

Setup: There needs to be enough space in the room for the whole group to walk around the furniture and around the perimeter of the room. If done outside, there needs to be space and a place to walk (parking lots will do as will lawns, sidewalks, or any open area).

Group Size: Any size group is fine.

Time: Five minutes. For the ten-minute version, increase the walking time, try some of the variations, and include a processing time at the end during which learners either talk about their Walkabout experience or write about it in their journals.

The Walkabout Instructions

- Direct learners to form standing pairs or triads. Tell them they are going to do a Walkabout in which they walk around the room, down the hall, or outside and back. On the first half of their journey, one person talks and the other listens. On the second half of the journey, the listener becomes the talker.
- Tell learners the length of time they have to do the Walkabout. From three to five minutes is usually enough time.
- Tell participants what they will be talking about as they do the Walkabout. Examples are how they can use what they've learned, the most important facts they remember from the material, questions they have, best practices they use pertaining to the topic, or a topic-related problem they want help with.
- As they do the Walkabout, you walk and observe, or you can join in and listen to a few of the walking discussions.
- Process the activity by asking the whole group what the most valuable takeaway from the activity was (some will say the exercise, others will say the chance to discuss the material or network with friends).

¡Tips and Variations!

Stretch and Breathe. If learners walk outside, remind them to stretch, breathe deeply, and enjoy the fresh air and sunshine.

Walkabout Parties. Learners do half of the Walkabout with their partners and then join up with another Walkabout pair to collaborate on ideas already shared.

Walkabout Reflections. Make a participant worksheet titled Walkabout Reflections or My Walkabout Journal. When the activity is over, invite participants to spend a few minutes writing about what they learned from the Walkabout. Their writing can include new information, action plans, questions they still have, or feelings about the activity.

Repeat It. Learners repeat the Walkabout during the training, deciding for themselves where to walk, the topic each time they walk, and what the results should be.

Create Your Own!

Think about other ways to do a Walkabout and jot them down here.

Blackout Bingo!

What Is Blackout Bingo?

With Blackout Bingo, each learner makes his own bingo card, fills in the bingo squares as directed by you, and then collects signatures from other participants by defining or by giving examples of his bingo card items. The point is to be one of the first to get a signature for every bingo item.

Blackout Bingo combines a conceptual review with physical exercise, friendly competition (even though it's possible for everyone to win), and a high-energy way to celebrate the learning. All in all, it's a great way to close a training session.

What Does Blackout Bingo Do?

Besides being a great review game, Blackout Bingo helps learners

- *Decide* what training concepts are really important to them.
- *Individualize* the training results by making their own bingo cards.
- *Define* training concepts in their own words.
- *Give* real-life examples of the information they learned in the training.
- *Choose* what they want to remember and use after the training is over.
- *Celebrate* the learning with a high-energy, connecting, closing activity.

 Getting Ready

Materials: Learners will need blank, standard-sized typing paper, pens or pencils, and small token prizes—one item per person. You will also need upbeat music, a boom box or other form of music player, and a small bag or box to hold the token prizes.

Setup: There needs to be enough physical space in the room for learners to be able to move and walk around the furniture while collecting signatures.

Group Size: For the activity to work best, the group needs to have at least a dozen people in it. The larger the group the better. Any maximum number of participants is fine.

Time: Five minutes. For the ten-minute version, increase the number of squares for items and signatures, do one of the activity variations, or extend the playing time so that all learners get a Blackout Bingo.

Blackout Bingo Instructions

• Direct each learner to fold a blank piece of paper into eight squares (for a shorter time limit, do four squares). In each square, they print a training concept that they consider important. They can also print information they plan to use when the training is over. There should be one concept or piece of information per bingo square. For example, in an auto shop class, a learner might write eight engine part names. In a beginning computer class, a learner might write eight computer terms, such as *boot up, download, browser, application, crash, DSL, hard drive,* and *USB port.*

• When they are finished filling in the squares, learners stand to show they are ready to play the game. Tell learners their goal is to get a different signature for each square item. Participants who get Blackout Bingo (that is, all squares filled with signatures) within a certain time limit win the game. A learner collects signatures by telling another person the definition of an item on her own card or by giving an example of an item. For example, Learner One's card has the words "active listening" written in a card square for a communication skills training. She pairs up with Learner Two and then defines the term. Learner Two signs Learner One's card square to indicate that she defined it correctly.

• While upbeat music plays, participants collect signatures. When each learner has a filled-in bingo card (that is, each item has a signature beside it), she waves her paper in the air, shouts "Blackout Bingo!" and runs up to the front of the room for a prize. You can have a few bingos, a majority of bingos, or all bingos depending upon the amount of time you give the training participants to collect signatures. About three minutes, or the average time it takes to play one song on the boom box, is usually enough.

• When the activity is over, tell learners to keep their Blackout Bingo cards as reminders of what they learned. They give each other high-fives, do a cheer, or applaud each other before they leave.

¡Tips and Variations!

Draw, Don't Fold. Learners draw the squares on the papers instead of folding them so that they can have six squares or ten squares. They can also label a square "free space" if you want them to have an odd number of squares.

Action Plans. Besides concepts or information learned, learners can write their action plans or next steps. In order to collect signatures, they have to explain their action plans to others. For example, on an eight-square card, a learner in a train-the-trainer class might write: "Study the trainer's manual, watch a pro, use a new activity, attend a workshop, read a book, use computer graphics, get a mentor, make a trainer's toolbox."

Training Challenges. Participants write topic-related challenges (for example, different kinds of difficult customers for a customer service training, or computer problems they might encounter for a technical training). In order to collect signatures, the person signing the card has to tell the cardholder how he would handle the challenge.

Burning Questions. Learners write topic-related questions, one per square. In order to collect signatures, the person signing the paper has to answer the question to the satisfaction of the cardholder.

One Signature per Minibreak. Do the game incrementally throughout the training day. After making their bingo cards by using a list of training concepts you've posted on a wall chart, learners gather signatures during sixty-second breaks spaced throughout the training. Either the cardholder has to define the term on his card in order to claim a signature, or the one signing the paper has to do the defining.

Bingo Home Play. If the training lasts more than one day, direct learners to take their cards home and collect signatures from family members and friends. The learner still has to define or give an example of the items on his card in order to collect the signatures. The signers will assume the learner's explanation is correct. The next day, participants bring their cards back for small prizes if they got a Blackout Bingo.

Create Your Own!

In the box below, write your own Blackout Bingo ideas.

Part Two

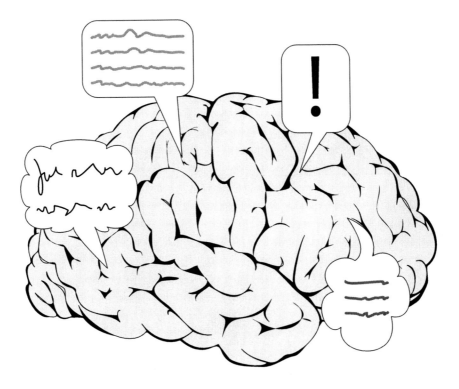

Heads Up!

Brain-Based Learning and Training

Quick Start

Mark-Up: Here are some of the concepts you will read about in Part Two of *The Ten-Minute Trainer*. Circle the words or phrases that sound familiar to you or that you think you can define. After reading the next few chapters, come back to this exercise and look over the list again. You will be able to circle all the terms then.

Recticular Activating System

Learning Compass

Making the Connections

Training Map

Practicing the Skills

Attention Breaker

Three Brains in One

Explaining the Concepts

Triune Brain

Celebrating the Learning

Attention Maker

Power-Hour Training Template

Television, with its emphasis on shorter informational segments and image-rich information delivery, gives us a major reason for changing our training methods. Another reason, and more important than television, has to do with how the human brain learns—a subject that is often neglected by many busy teachers and trainers. Why? Because it takes time to read through all the studies about the human brain—and time to figure out how to apply that research to tomorrow's training.

But what if we had access to a simplified version of some of the brain research? Better yet, what if we could put it to use immediately to design and deliver our next training? It would be worth it, then, to take time in our busy schedules to read the research.

Part Two of *The Ten-Minute Trainer* does just that. It will give you practical ways of using three important pieces of brain research about learning. You may be familiar with these concepts, or they may be new to you. Either way, you'll discover useful insights about how people learn and what to do about it in your own teaching.

The Learning Brain

The human brain is a phenomenally efficient, and imminently adaptable, learning tool. How it manages to learn as much as it does as fast as it does still amazes the researchers who study it.

Not only is the brain designed to learn, *it can't help but learn!* That is its basic function—to make sense out of the world around it. It is a pattern-seeking device, always hunting for the mosaic pieces of its world, which it can then combine in infinite ways to create its own artistic masterpiece of what reality is, according to the patterns it has identified.

Patterns can be physical cycles of the natural world (for example, birth and death, the four seasons, or positions of stars in the night sky), experiential (such as the sequence of movements in a dance, or the cultural norms and routines taught to a child from the time he is born), cognitive (language and mathematics are two examples), affective (emotional responses to pain or pleasure), as well as everything else the human brain is capable of learning.

Besides being programmed to learn, *the human brain likes to learn!* Whether the feeling of pleasure comes from the brain's release of endorphins or from the human spirit's desire to self-actualize, the fact remains: *left to itself, without outside interference, the human brain always chooses to learn—directed only by its own needs, desires, curiosity, or strong emotions.*

As trainers, the question we need to ask is: Why, in the formal learning environment of the classroom or training room, is it assumed that learners must be coerced (bribed, threatened, convinced, ordered, told, directed) to learn?

The answer is twofold and may surprise you. First, most formal methods of learning aren't based on how the human brain learns. Instead they are based primarily on tradition ("It has always been done this way"), as well as on issues such as control, time, type of material to be covered, and situational constraints (group size, room setup, curriculum directives, and the like).

136

The human ego often plays a role in the formal learning environment as well: the teacher or "subject matter expert" is perceived to be the one with all the knowledge, authority, and power within the small confines of a classroom. Regardless of whether this perception is accurate, many subject matter experts end up believing it is and acting accordingly.

The second reason we assume that people must be made to learn in a formal learning environment is that the human brain willingly keeps its attention focused on only what holds its interest. A person (no matter what the age) will always turn his attention to whatever is important *to him*, not to what someone else says is important. Again, importance has to do with a person's own needs, desires, curiosity, or emotion. For the sake of simplicity, we'll list the first three words under the fourth: emotion. So in formal classes and training, where the course content is often irrelevant or boring to the learner, the human brain must be convinced, in some way, that it needs to pay attention.

Emotion Directs Attention, Which Directs Learning

Let's face it—no one likes to be told what to learn. Encouraged, maybe. But *we* want to choose the content and the learning methods. *The desire to explore what interests us in the world around us, in our own time and own way, is basic to the human brain.*

When we, as trainers, understand the brain research about learning, and we know what drives learning (emotion), then we can create learning experiences that are compatible with how the brain learns, rather than using methods that only tire and frustrate it.

The brain research in Part Two illustrates the power of emotion in determining what our learners will pay attention to, what they won't, and what they'll finally end up learning. The research helps us deepen our understanding of the learning–teaching process. It offers us effective, brain-based alternatives to traditional training design and delivery. It also validates this book's two major concepts: *shorter segments of instruction are better than longer ones, and learners remember more when they are involved in the learning.*

Overview of Part Two

Part Two begins with the brain's Attention Maker, also called the Reticular Activating System. This part of the brain plays a critical role in deciding what will hold the learner's attention, and what won't. Emotions—needs, desires, curiosity—are the keys to what the Attention Maker notices.

Next, Part Two explores the significance of the Three Brains in One, also called the Triune Brain. This research illustrates how important the feeling of psychological safety is in a learning experience, and how to create that feeling of safety through learner-to-learner connections and involvement.

After that, you'll discover the Learning Compass, also called Learning the Natural Way. This is the foundation piece of all human learning, whether the person doing the learning knows it or not.

From the Learning Compass comes the Training Map. The Training Map is a four-step training model for designing and delivering learning experiences based on how people naturally learn. As an added bonus, the Learning Compass and Training Map will also help you manage your design and delivery time more efficiently. Together, these two tools will be powerful additions to your own expertise as a training professional.

Finally, Part Two gives you five Power-Hour Training Templates and an example of how to use the templates to show you how easy it is to apply the concepts included in both Parts One and Two.

Wrapping It Up

Ultimately, Part Two is all about learning—how we learn, what keeps us learning, what happens when we don't learn, and how to use this information to help our training participants learn. The more we as professional educators and trainers know about how the human brain learns, the better we can do what we do—and the better off our learners will be for it.

These concepts are not all-inclusive, that is, they are only a small portion of the brain research about human learning that is available to us now. For a more in-depth look at the research, see the Remarkable Resources in the back of the book.

My dear boy, all you need to know is that
your brain has a mind of its own.

—Herman Herkemeier III

———♟———

Early to Finish

Mark-Up. As you read through the next few chapters, jot down any thoughts, reactions, questions, or comments you have in the margins of the pages. Highlight the important sentences—those that you want to remember. Flag the important pages. Draw a doodle or two. Make the concepts your own by marking them in some way so that you can find them more easily and remember them longer. When you are done reading Part Two, go back to the Quick Start at the beginning of this introduction, and finish the exercise.

Attention Maker, Attention Breaker

The Reticular Activating System and Learning

Quick Start

Think and Write: Name six things you already do to keep your participants awake, alert, and interested while they learn. Jot them down in the space below.

Now name four things you could change in your training so that your learners become even more motivated to learn. Jot these down in the space below.

After you finish reading this chapter, add two new ideas to the ones you've listed.

Picture This

You're sitting in a half-day workshop dealing with a new financial software package for your company. You listen for awhile and then your mind begins to drift as you think about all the errands you need to run after the workshop ends. Suddenly you realize you haven't even heard a word of the lecture for the past thirty minutes—you couldn't repeat one thing the instructor, Marie, said if your life depended on it.

What just happened? A part of your brain—about the size of your little finger—took over. This small but mighty brain part said to your conscious mind, "Been here, done this. I can handle it. You can take a hike." And that's exactly what your conscious mind did. It busied itself with other thoughts as you sat listening to the lecture. All the while, this tiny piece of gray matter was screening out sensory data—sights, sounds, textures, smells, movement—that it considered unimportant, including the sound of the instructor's voice.

Without warning, Marie says something that catches the attention of your drifting mind: "When I throw this ball at you, please tell the group one important fact they need to remember about this software package, then toss the ball to someone else." You are instantly alert again, as you watch her toss a soft toy ball out to the group. Fortunately for you, someone else catches it and states a fact about the software program. As the group tosses the ball around the room, you remain alert, just in case the ball gets tossed your way.

What happened now? The tiny part of your brain that was busy screening out sensory data panicked because something in the environment had changed. It mentally shouted to your conscious mind, "Wake up and pay attention! Something is different and you need to be here." Your conscious mind instantly came back to the present, assessed the situation, and decided how to handle it.

What Is the RAS and What Does It Do?

This pinky-sized area of the brain has a scientific name: the reticular activating system (RAS). A more common name for it is the Attention Maker. It is located near the brainstem (survival brain)—the part of your brain that controls the fight-or-flight response. It sends electronic signals from your brainstem through the limbic or emotional brain to your cerebrum (thinking brain).

The Attention Maker has two specific jobs: it "makes" or "breaks" attention. The first job is to make your thinking brain pay attention to what is going on in the environment. The second job is to break or stop your thinking brain's attention to the environment, causing the cerebrum to go on "automatic pilot," that is, to do certain actions automatically while thinking of other things.

The Attention Maker does both jobs by screening the sensory data coming into your brain from the brainstem. Then it decides what data is important enough to send along electronic circuits to the cerebrum. When the important sensory information reaches your thinking brain, you suddenly become conscious of specific sights, sounds, movements, smells, textures, and the like that are around you.

If the Attention Maker decides that the sensory information is not that important, it will stop the electronic messages to your thinking brain, effectively screening out the sensory data so that you don't see, hear, or otherwise notice unimportant things.

Picture a security officer (the RAS) standing at the entrance to an important bank (the cerebrum) with a long line of prospective clients (sensory data) waiting to get in. The security officer screens each client's request and says, "Yes, you may go on in. No, you have to wait out here. Yes, you're important enough to step inside. No, you're not important enough to enter right now."

Time and Energy

You have experienced the attention-breaker activity of the RAS thousands of times. For example, you no longer consciously hear repetitive sounds you're used to: the traffic noise outside the window, the hum of the refrigerator, the clock chiming the hours, the radio station in the background. You don't consciously notice the hallway photos, the tree in your front yard, your office furniture, the elevator music, or the billboards by the highway.

You have also experienced the attention-maker activity of the RAS. Because it subconsciously monitors all sensory information in the environment around you, it notices any changes in that stimuli. Doing something about the changes is not its job. So it simply alerts the thinking brain that full consciousness is now required and that being on automatic pilot will no longer work. Suddenly you become aware of a fire engine wail, a radio announcement about a traffic accident, an unfamiliar car parked outside your home, or a suspicious person lurking next to your office building.

The cerebrum needs the RAS to screen sensory data in order to save you both time and energy. Let's explore these two ideas a little further.

It takes a great deal of mental energy to be consciously aware of all the sensory stimulation around you. It also takes energy to decide what, if anything, to do about all the sensory data. The thinking brain can save itself a great deal of energy by not consciously paying attention to every sight, sound, touch, taste, smell, movement, and so forth.

It also takes time to consciously process all that sensory data. If the cerebrum had to notice and then had to decide how to respond to everything in the environment in any given moment, simple tasks could take hours to complete.

For example, just think about how many physical actions are involved in something as simple as brushing your teeth. It would be extraordinarily time-consuming to have to think through and make a decision about each of those actions. So once the cerebrum learns how to do the task, it assigns the sequence of actions to the Attention Maker, much like an airplane pilot who decides to turn on the automatic pilot switch so that the plane flies itself. Anytime you do anything familiar and repetitive—washing dishes, taking a shower, getting dressed, exercising, gardening, sleeping—the RAS takes over the physical actions, thus freeing the cerebrum to think of other things.

Driving is the most understood example of what it feels like to be on automatic pilot. When you first learned how to drive, you had to be completely conscious of everything around you. Now, most likely, after having driven for years, you pull into the parking lot at work in the morning not even consciously aware of how you got there. Driving has become such a repetitive task that when you back out of your driveway, the RAS immediately begins screening out all the sensory details related to driving that you're familiar with.

By the way, besides alerting the cerebrum to any changes in the environment, the RAS also sends signals that have to do with physical need (example: waking up from a deep sleep in order to go to the bathroom), self-made choice (example: deciding to buy a red car and suddenly seeing red cars everywhere), and hearing or seeing your own name. It is also responsible for heightening sensory acuteness in the case of survival situations (example: the sudden sharpening of your sense of hearing when you become aware of an unfamiliar sound in the middle of the night).

Learning, Teaching, and the RAS

The reticular activating system is crucial to directing and maintaining a learner's attention, regardless of whether the learning takes place in formal places such as classrooms or in real-life situations such as on-the-job training.

Whenever a learning environment or procedure becomes routine, that is, familiar and repetitive, the RAS takes on the role of Attention Breaker. It breaks the learner's conscious concentration and gives his thinking brain permission to muse about things unrelated to the task at hand, which in this case is sitting in a classroom listening to someone teach.

When anything changes from what is familiar in a learning environment, the RAS becomes the Attention Maker. It directs the learner's thinking brain to consciously pay attention to what is going on around him, including listening to the teacher.

The importance of this for us as trainers is clear: *When we want our learners to pay close, conscious attention to important information, we have to catch the attention of the RAS by changing something in the environment.*

Changes That Engage the RAS

First, we can change things that have to do with our own instructional methods. For example, we can

- *Vary* the tone, speed, loudness, or softness of our own voice.
- *Move* around the room as we talk.
- *Gesture* while we speak, using hand and arm movements and facial expressions.
- *Act out* a story to illustrate important concepts.
- *Ask* a question and then pause for five full seconds (most trainers only wait for two seconds or less before answering their own question).
- *Add* humor with a topic-related joke or anecdote.
- *Use* topic-related, visual images while we talk—photos, cartoons, drawings, and so forth.

We can also change the activities we use to involve learners. Learners can

- *Participate* in short, quick, review activities (any of the 150 activities in Part One will increase learner participation).
- *Stand* and stretch if they have been sitting awhile.
- *Walk* outside or around the room with a friend while discussing what they've learned.
- *Take* notes a number of different ways while listening to the lecture.
- *Draw* images to represent what they've learned.
- *Write* topic-related comments on wall charts.
- *Discuss* a question about the lecture material.
- *Make* a quick review game with index cards.
- *Quiz* each other about what they've learned.

Last, we can change the physical room environment. We can

- *Move* chairs into clustered groups instead of straight rows.
- *Use* round tables for small group work.
- *Have* a break-out space for large group activities.
- *Set aside* a reading and study area with cushions, pillows, or comfortable chairs.
- *Rearrange* desks into small cluster groups.
- *Add* aromas that please most people (apples, cinnamon, citrus).
- *Play* music that either energizes or relaxes learners.
- *Provide* snacks and beverages on occasion (learners can bring them too).
- *Get rid* of anything that is aesthetically unpleasing (exposed wires, broken furniture, discarded paper).
- *Decorate* the walls with colorful wall charts, hangings, mobiles, streamers, and learner-made projects.
- *Create* colorful centerpieces for each table with colored paper, confetti, hard candy, toys, and the like.
- *Make* sure the room looks and feels warm, inviting, and interesting.

Wrapping It Up

The learning strategies and training methods to keep learners' reticular activating systems engaged are limited only by our own beliefs about teaching and learning.

If we have the perception that learning takes place when we talk and learners listen, we will probably deliver most of our information in lecture-type formats. If that's the case, we run the risk of creating for our learners what we have too often experienced (and what the beginning of this chapter described)—a learning environment in which the learners' conscious minds slip away even if they seem to be listening.

If we understand the importance of the RAS in training, we will change our instructional methods and learning activities regularly to accommodate the Attention Maker's need for stimulation. We will accept that, in order to really learn something (as opposed to just hearing it), the conscious mind must be fully and completely present. Later, the cerebrum may hand a physical or mental skill over to the RAS once the skill has been mastered (for example, performing a reoccurring safety procedure, running a daily computer program, repeating the same verbal customer service information). But in the learning stage, the Attention Maker must engage the thinking brain. And the best way to make sure that happens is to include regular changes in both our instructional methods and the activities we use to involve learners.

The number one reason we forget is because we aren't paying attention in the first place.

—Lynn Stern

Early to Finish

Action Plan. Review the lists under "Changes That Engage the RAS" and circle four changes you can make that you haven't yet tried. Make a commitment to experiment with these changes in your next training.

Three Brains in One

The Triune Brain and Learning

Quick Start

Think and Write: Write a word or phrase defining the term or stating its importance in learning and training.

1. Brainstem, subcortex _____

2. Limbic system _____

3. Cerebrum, neocortex _____

4. Downshifting _____

5. Safety _____

6. Learning community _____

After reading this chapter, read the definitions you've written above and see whether the context of what you wrote matches the context of what you've learned. If not, don't worry—just go ahead and change your answers to match the research. That's called a "mediated learning experience," in which what you first knew is changed by what you later learned.

Picture This

You and a friend have decided to take a basic computer course at your local community college. As you walk across the campus, you begin to feel excited. You've enjoyed taking other college classes. You like the college environment. You have a certain degree of confidence because you understand general computer technology. And your past experiences with formal learning have, for the most part, been positive.

Your friend's feelings differ from yours. He has not had as many successes with schools, classrooms, or technology. In fact, if truth be told, he often felt like a failure as a child in school. Consequently, he is somewhat reluctantly taking this course with you. He's already making mental excuses for dropping out if the course is too difficult. His nervousness and discomfort increase as he approaches the building.

You and your friend enter the classroom together with very different mindsets toward this new learning experience. How much each of you learns will largely depend upon your mental attitudes and emotional states as you walk into the room.

From Parts to Whole

In his book *Human Brain and Human Learning* (1983), author Leslie Hart cited the research done by Paul MacLean, the former director of the Brain and Behavior Laboratory of the United States National Institute of Mental Health. MacLean theorized that the physical human brain evolved over centuries into three somewhat distinct parts, all interconnected and all playing an important role in learning and memory.

In order to simplify MacLean's theory and to understand it in both a kinesthetic (movement) and a spatial (image-rich) way, you are going to use your own hands to represent your three brains in one.

Make a fist with one hand and hold it in front of you. Your fist represents your brain sitting on top of your spinal cord (your arm). With your other hand, touch your wrist. Your wrist represents the brainstem, also called the subcortex or survival brain, located at the base of your head. It's the part that is primarily responsible for safety, and it triggers the fight–flight reaction to any perceived danger, either physical or psychological.

Now touch your fist. Your fist represents the limbic or emotional brain, located in the middle of your head. It is the part that houses most emotions and that moves information and experiences with strong emotional connections into long-term memory.

Finally, lay your other hand over your fist as if it is covering it. This represents the cerebrum, neocortex, or thinking brain. It is the gray matter, the newspaper-sized portion of the brain (if it were stretched flat) that is squashed into a small space (which accounts for its convoluted folds). It has two sides (hemispheres) with a complex wiring of connections (corpus callosum) between the two. It is the part that most photos show.

The Downshifting Brain

In any new learning experience, whenever you feel threatened, your brain begins to "downshift," that is, the thinking brain shuts down (take away the hand covering your fist), and the emotional and survival parts of the brain take over (continue to hold your fist in front of you and wiggle it). The threat could be physical (the room is too hot, too cold, you're hungry or thirsty, or there could be a perceived danger from another person or from the environment). The threat could also be psychological (you're afraid of being humiliated in front of your peers, of asking a stupid question, of being ridiculed, of failure).

If the perceived threat is severe enough, the survival brain kicks in with the fight–flight response and you "wig out," that is, you become so mentally and emotionally uncomfortable that most learning stops (circle your fist vigorously in the air to represent wigging out). At this point, you automatically respond to the discomfort by becoming either verbally or physically defensive (fighting) or by not participating or literally leaving the room (fleeing).

In reality you *can* learn some things while downshifting into survival brain. Your brain will do whatever it needs to do to ensure your survival, including learning what it needs to learn in order to get you out of a dangerous situation. And to make sure you don't place yourself in harm's way again, *your brain will warn you in the future whenever you experience any situation similar to the painful one.* It does this by lumping all sensory data together into a memory packet labeled "Danger." All the sensory data—sights, sounds, smells, movement, textures—that were around you when you were in fight–flight mode become part of the danger packet and, according to your brain, are to be avoided in the future.

The implications of this for learning and teaching are profound. Most wounded learners—folks who have had negative experiences with teachers, classrooms, peers, or schools—avoid things that remind them of that pain: classes, workshops, training, desks, blackboards, textbooks, instructors, and trainers. When these wounded learners have to attend a class or training, they downshift before they even arrive because of the warnings that are sounding in their heads. *They walk into the room already in a fight–flight state.* Their brain is already planning to do whatever it needs to do to get them out of there.

Another even more important implication for learning is this: *training participants can downshift while the training is going on as well.* Any physical or psychological discomfort will trigger the beginning stages of downshifting. *When discomfort increases, learning decreases.*

Put the representation of your brain back together again: hold up your fist and lay your other hand over it. When you have all three parts of your brain working together like this, optimum learning can take place. *The key to making this happen is a learning experience that is safe, both physically and psychologically.* The name of the game is safety.

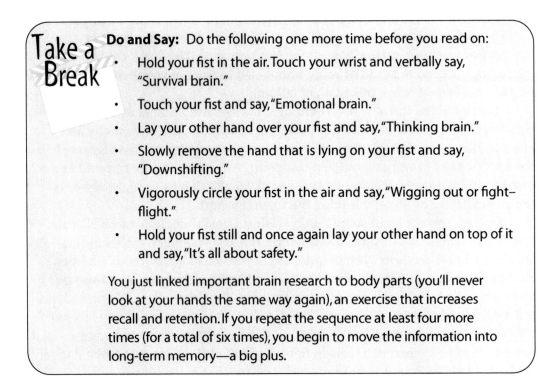

Take a Break

Do and Say: Do the following one more time before you read on:

- Hold your fist in the air. Touch your wrist and verbally say, "Survival brain."
- Touch your fist and say, "Emotional brain."
- Lay your other hand over your fist and say, "Thinking brain."
- Slowly remove the hand that is lying on your fist and say, "Downshifting."
- Vigorously circle your fist in the air and say, "Wigging out or fight–flight."
- Hold your fist still and once again lay your other hand on top of it and say, "It's all about safety."

You just linked important brain research to body parts (you'll never look at your hands the same way again), an exercise that increases recall and retention. If you repeat the sequence at least four more times (for a total of six times), you begin to move the information into long-term memory—a big plus.

From Connections to Community

The quickest and most powerful way to create safety in a training is to connect learners with each other, with the topic, and with you in positive, fun, low-risk ways. Furthermore, the connections need to be woven throughout the learning experience, not just thrown in at the beginning and then forgotten. By encouraging learners to interact, appreciate each other, and learn from each other, you're creating a learning community, that is, a group of people who interact in positive ways and who are emotionally invested in helping each other learn.

A safe learning community means that learners can make mistakes and learn from them. They can ask all kinds of questions and not be afraid of sounding stupid. They can disagree and not be put down. They will not feel threatened either physically or psychologically. And they will have opportunities to learn in ways that support their own needs and desires.

A safe learning community also means that you, the trainer, can also make mistakes. You don't have to be perfect. You don't have to have all the answers. You can change what doesn't work and polish what does work. You can adjust the training to fit the needs of the learners, even while the training is going on. Best of all, you can be yourself—authentic, honest, and uniquely you. You will not feel threatened either physically or psychologically. You can give it your personal best and know that your best is enough.

In a safe learning community, learners always treat each other with more tolerance, patience, humor, and compassion—as opposed to a class where individuals are strangers to each other and where no personal, meaningful connections take place.

Techniques Are Never Value-Neutral

Two important concepts to keep in mind when creating safe learning communities are

• *You teach who you are and what you value.* You can't help it. It would be like stepping out of your own skin to do otherwise. Who you are—your own unique spirit, personality traits, energy—shines through every word you say, everything you do, every decision you make. What you value about life and learning will also shine through and give a message, consciously or not, about what's OK and not OK.

• *The instructional techniques you choose to use—or not—also reflect your deepest values.* In spite of the old myth that it's inappropriate to teach values in a class or training, you can't help but do exactly that. Every choice you make, including which training activities to use, are values-based choices. How you set up a training room (for example, chairs in theater-style rows versus chairs in small cluster groups) will give a message about what you value. The activities your learners engage in (for example, individual versus cooperative versus competitive) also send a message. There's no judgment about any of this—it just is.

When you're aware that your training design and delivery choices reflect who you are and what you value, you begin to look at your choices with a different mindset, and you may change some of your decisions.

For example, you may think you value the creation of a learning community, but you choose to lecture almost exclusively. Whether you mean it or not, the subconscious message of this choice is: "I'm the expert so I get to talk. Learners are not experts so they get to listen." You value your expertise more than what your learners may already know about the topic. Once you realize the covert message of this solo instructional method, you can change it to include more learner involvement.

Another example: when your learners do interact, you have them play only highly competitive games. Again, whether you mean to or not, the message is clear: "Winning is good, losing is bad. It's not about learning—it's about winning." You value competition more than cooperation. You can change this hidden message by including some cooperative activities.

A final example: you want learners to learn from each other but you never give them time to discuss the material among themselves. You may subconsciously feel that small group discussions are a waste of training time. Change this mindset by adding a few sixty-second activities to your training until you see for yourself the value of learner involvement and discussion.

Take a Break

Matchup: On another sheet of paper, write down two or three instructional techniques that you use regularly. Beside them, jot down what personal value you are expressing by including each technique.

Technique I Use	I Value
For example:	You might write:
1. Giving learners quiet time to think and write.	1. Individualized, thoughtful reflection.
2. Having learners move around a lot.	2. Physical activity while learning.
3. Whole group discussions.	3. The give and take of information.

Just becoming aware of the values that guide your training decisions is a big step—and one that will help you choose your instructional strategies with care.

Building the Learning Community

So how do you go about creating a learning community where everyone feels both physically and psychologically safe enough to learn together, make mistakes, ask questions, and disagree?

Here are a number of ideas to get you started.

Renew the Room. If possible, change the physical environment to support what you value and what you know learners need. Rearrange the furniture so that small groups can work together, check the temperature, decorate the room to make it interesting and inviting, provide snacks and beverages when you can, and allow for regular breaks.

Social Suggestions. Have a few (no more than three or four) community suggestions posted on the wall where they can be seen as reminders. They can be simple: *Listen before talking. No putdowns. Share time and materials. Be open to new ideas.* Or have the learners create the list with suggestions they feel are relevant, and post their list. By the way, never assume that just because a group of people work together they also feel psychologically safe with each other. Safety has to be built into a training every time a group of learners gets together.

Walk Your Talk. You have to model the community behaviors you want your learners to use. For example: if one suggestion is "No putdowns" (because friendly teasing in this fashion can often quickly cross the line into hurtful teasing), then you have to practice what you preach. Another example: if you want learners to listen to you and to each other, you have to do the same—you have to listen to them.

Sixty-Second Connections. Connections are not just opening activities. Nor are they icebreakers, which are simply social activities designed to help learners get to know each other. Connections are structured activities that give learners opportunities to engage in dialogue about the training material and what is important to them. In other words, these activities consistently connect learners to each other, to the material, and to you in safe and thought-provoking ways. *Connections build learning communities.* Use the 150 activities in Part One so that learner-to-learner connections are woven into the fabric of the training time.

Mix Them Up. At times, randomly sort training participants so that they get to know many people in the training and not just their friends or the one or two people seated beside them. You can direct learners to form different pairs or groups for many of the activities in Part One, and you can periodically change the mixture of the seated groups as well.

Take the Pulse. Be aware of the emotional overtones of the learning group. Is there tension or does everyone seem relaxed? Are there intense discussions or angry comments? Are putdowns being used a lot, or sarcasm, which is always disguised anger? Differing opinions and disagreement are good. Personal attacks are not. Deal with problems privately first. For example, at a break you might talk one-on-one with a sarcastic person to help that person choose a different behavior. You can also address the problem in general with the whole group: "It feels as though there is a great deal of tension in the room right now. What is going on? What can we do to make it be a more positive learning environment?" Spend a few minutes identifying the issue and then reaching a consensus about what to do.

Safety First. Never sacrifice the group for the individual. Sometimes you have to literally let go of a training participant in order to keep the group psychologically safe. That may mean asking a difficult participant to leave or giving him a choice of leaving (if he continues to display negative behavior) or staying (if he decides to behave in more positive ways).

Ask for Feedback. Periodically ask for learner feedback—written anonymously—about the strength of the learning community: "How does it feel to you to be a part of this group? What is working well? What is a suggestion to make it work better?"

Pleasure, Not Pain

Writer Alfred Mercier once said: "What we learn with pleasure, we never forget."

Author and corporate trainer Bob Pike put it another way: "Learning is directly proportional to the amount of fun we are having."

When learners participate in meaningful, pleasurable, low-risk activities that connect them to each other and to the concepts being presented, they form a strong learning community and they increase their ability to remember the information longer. Their minds move the learning into the emotional center of the limbic or emotional brain, where long-term memories are stored.

The words *pleasure* and *fun* are not synonymous with *easy*. Learning can be challenging and intense without being painful. The difference is one of chemicals: the brain directs the release of pleasure chemicals called endorphins when learning is fun, and stress chemicals such as adrenalin when learning is a threat. All emotions move learning to the limbic brain, but pleasurable emotions entice the brain to remember and repeat what caused the pleasure, whereas painful emotions warn the brain to stay away from whatever caused the pain. In other words, any pleasant learning experience will usually cause learners to want more of what created the positive feelings: more classes, training, instruction, and connections with teachers, trainers, and other learners.

Back to the Beginning

Let's return to the scene at the beginning of this chapter, where you and your friend walk into the computer class—you eagerly, your friend fearfully. You both sit down. The instructor begins with a sixty-second Pair Share in which all participants turn to people seated next to them, introduce themselves, and state why they are there and what they hope to learn. Your friend begins talking to a stranger on his left.

Then the instructor leads the class in a five-minute Take a Stand activity. People who love computers or who are technologically experienced stand on one side of the room. Those who hate computers or have little experience with them stand on the other side. You stand on one side, your friend on the other. What is surprising is that your friend is not alone. The class is pretty evenly divided and you can tell by the look on your friend's face that he is feeling better about being there.

As the activity progresses, and both sides share their computer hopes or fears, your friend relaxes even more. Gone is the tension caused by downshifting. Now he joins in the conversation and almost seems comfortable with the class.

Even though it's a computer class, the instructor makes sure learners connect with each other in a variety of quick, interesting ways throughout the morning. Soon the more experienced are mentoring the less experienced. All feel good about being there and are satisfied with what they are learning.

At the end of the class, learners state what they plan to do with what they learned. Handshakes and applause end the session. As you and your friend leave the building, he turns to you with a smile on his face and asks, "When is the next computer class?"

Wrapping It Up

The human brain is hard wired to keep us both physically and psychologically safe. All three parts of the brain—survival brain, emotional brain, and thinking brain—work together best when the need for safety is met in a class or training.

As you have learned, one of the surest ways to create a feeling of emotional safety is by connecting learners to each other and to the content in fun, safe ways. When you include a variety of ways learners can make those connections throughout a training, you create a safe learning community for the duration of the learning experience.

*It's simple . . . we either get used to thinking about
the subtle processes of learning and
sharing knowledge in transient networks,
or we perish.*

—Tom Peters

Early to Finish

Think and Write. Go back to the Quick Start at the beginning of this chapter and follow the instructions to finish that activity. Then skim the Remarkable Resources in the back of the book and highlight any of the brain research books that sound interesting to you.

Let the Compass Be Your Guide

The Learning Compass and Learning the Natural Way

Quick Start

Place Your Order: Think about something you want to learn how to do that you haven't done before. Put the following list in numerical order (1–4) depending upon what would come first, second, third, and fourth for you as you learn this new skill, activity, or subject.

_____ I will practice everyday until I get good at it.

_____ I will read a topic-related book, watch a movie, take a class, or sign up for lessons.

_____ I will decide why I want to learn how to do it and what I will do once I learn it.

_____ I will talk to others about it, find out what they know, and maybe watch them do it.

As you read this chapter, think about how you approach any new learning experience and what steps you take when you learn something new. Then think about your training participants and how you structure their learning experiences.

In this chapter, you'll discover the four steps most people take when learning anything new, and the order those four steps usually follow.

Picture This

You decide to learn a new sport, one that provides fresh air and exercise, even as it challenges your mind. The sport you choose is golf. Besides the exercise and mental challenge, you also choose golf because you like watching the game on television and because some of your friends play golf and have invited you to join them. (Note: If you already know how to play golf, think back to when you first learned the sport. If you have no interest in golf, substitute another sport and read this section with it in mind.)

After making the decision to learn this sport, you realize that you already know a bit about golfing from your TV viewing. You know some of the terms as well as how a good golf swing should look. You know a little about the different types of clubs that golfers use, as well as the game's scoring system.

Now what are the next steps you decide to take? Read the following three bulleted sentences and then number them 2, 3, 4, in the order that you would do them:

- You tell your golfing friends about your decision, listen to their golf stories, and get advice about how to get started.

- You rent a golf movie, read a how-to book on golf, or sign up for lessons from an expert.

- You go out to a putting green, rent a club and some golf balls, and practice— making mistakes and learning from them. Later you take some lessons.

Regardless of the numbered order of the preceding three sentences, you will probably do all of the activities they describe at some point while learning to play golf. In other words, what you will be experiencing as you become a golfer is a natural process of learning: deciding to learn the sport, finding out what you already know and what others know, listening to the experts, practicing the skills you need, and finally getting good enough to be able to play golf with your friends, which was your goal to begin with.

This learning process is as natural to human beings as breathing. We experience this process whenever we learn anything new. The point is that when we know *how* we learn, we can then use this knowledge to design effective learning experiences for others.

The Natural Cycle of Learning

In his book *Experiential Learning* (1984), David Kolb, a Case Western Reserve University professor, coined the term "the natural cycle of learning" to describe four common phases or steps of the learning process. Kolb observed that when a person first decides to learn, he draws on his own prior experience (what he already knows), as well as the experiences of others (what they already know). Then the learner seeks out the new information he needs and learns from the experts by taking classes, lessons, or learning from a mentor. He studies or practices what he has learned. Finally, he puts it all together—both the old and the new—and uses it in some way in his own life.

Kolb called the first step in this learning cycle the "concrete experience" phase: a person learns from real-life experiences and then draws on those experiences, and his feelings about them, in order to learn something new. Kolb noted that all learning begins and ends with the learner himself. Learning new information comes only after the learner has figured out what he wants to learn, what he already knows about it, and what he needs to know that he doesn't yet know.

Kolb named the second step in the cycle the "reflective observation" phase: a person thinks about what he knows and what others know about the topic or skill being learned. In other words, the learner talks with others about what they already know, listens to them, and thinks about what they say.

Kolb labeled the third step the "abstract conceptualization" phase: a person learns the new information he is seeking and combines it with what he, and others, already know. At this point, he may turn to a subject matter expert, a mentor, or a professional who will teach him what he needs to know.

Kolb called the fourth step the "active experimentation" phase: a person uses the new learning in some way—solving problems, creating something new, or changing something in his own life to demonstrate what he has learned. Kolb emphasized that real learning always leads to some form of action.

The golf example in this chapter illustrated these four phases or steps of the natural cycle of learning. Everything you've learned, both as a child and as an adult, has included these four steps: you decided to learn something and figured out what you already knew about it; you learned what others knew about it; you found someone to teach you more; you studied it, practiced it, and finally used it in your own life. As a child, you learned to read or ride a bicycle. As a teenager, you may have learned to speak another language or drive a car. As an adult, you probably learned to do your taxes or use a computer. Whatever you were learning to do, you experienced this natural cycle of learning, whether or not you were aware of it.

In order to make this natural learning process useful to us as trainers, we are going to call this cycle Learning the Natural Way, and we are going to use the metaphor of a compass with its four directional points to indicate the four steps of the cycle. This will help simplify Kolb's research so that we can both remember it and use it in practical ways when we teach and train.

What Is the Learning Compass and What Does It Do?

For any physical journey, a navigational compass—with its directional coordinates of north, east, south, and west—is one of the most powerful tools we can carry with us. With a compass to guide us, we make sure that we won't get lost and that we can ultimately find our way home.

The same applies to a learning journey: we can use a metaphoric compass with its four directional points representing the four steps in Learning the Natural Way. The Learning Compass will guide us home; that is, it will guide us in the direction of our learning goals.

For us as trainers, this compass is a reminder that everyone learns this way, including those we teach. More important, it forms the foundation for the Training Map described in the next chapter. To understand how to use the Training Map, we must first understand the Learning Compass.

Here is an overview of the Learning Compass and its directional points that represent the four steps in Learning the Natural Way (you are already familiar with these steps):

- *North represents self.* Here, the learner decides what information or skill she wants to learn, why she wants to learn it, and what she already knows and has experienced related to the subject.

- *East represents others.* Here, the learner finds out what other people know about the subject. These people may be family, friends, community members, coworkers, teachers, or other learners in the learning experience itself. The learner links what she knows with what they know.

- *South represents information.* Here, the learner begins to gather new information to add to what she (and others) know. She may gather this information a number of different ways: through books, videos, courses, meetings, real-life experiences, college classes, the Internet, self-study programs, lessons, training, mentoring, apprenticeships, and the like.

- *West represents action.* Here, the learner puts the new knowledge to use, practices a skill, or does something with what she has learned. This is where all learning leads: to action, a completion of a goal (and probably the creation of a new one), the desired outcome, or the end result.

All real learning—when something is learned, remembered, and used in some fashion—is a journey that includes these four steps: self, others, information, and action. They might not always occur in that order, but they are always present whenever a person learns the natural way. The four compass points are metaphoric memory aids for the four steps: north–self, east–others, south–information, west–action.

Again, think of something you recently learned. Go over the learning process in your mind and you will recognize these four steps. Say, for example, that you recently decided to invest some money in the stock market. You made the decision based on your desire to see your money increase in value (north–self). You already knew some things about investing from reading the newspaper and talking with friends and family members about it (east–others). You decided to attend an investment class at the local community college, or maybe you subscribed to an investment magazine that would teach you what you needed to know (south–information). You joined an Internet investment service and practiced buying and selling some small stocks until you felt comfortable with the process. Then you created your own stock portfolio and began seriously working at increasing its value (west–action). As with the golf example, you can see how your investment journey also followed the same four steps in Learning the Natural Way.

Helping Others Learn the Natural Way

Let's bring Learning the Natural Way into your training room. Remind yourself of the four compass points and what they represent: north–self, east–others, south–information, west–action. Then do some of the following to ensure that you've included the four steps in your training:

- *Give* learners time to talk about or write down what they want to learn (north–self). Use the Quick Start Time Sponges or Connection activities in Part One to do this.

- *Point out* the WIIFM—What's in It for Me?—that is, what learners will get out of the training (north–self). You can state these goals verbally or post them where everyone can read them.

- *Allow* learners time to discuss with other learners what they already know about the topic (east–others). Use the Quick Start, Connection, Gallery Walk, or Shout Out activities in Part One.

- *Encourage* learners to ask questions of you and of each other, either in verbal or written form (east–others). Use the Pair Shares or Think and Write activities in Part One.

- *Have* learners take notes during the lecture segments of the training (south–information). Use Think and Writes and Mark-Ups in Part One, or Graphic Organizers from "What's a Picture Worth?" in Part Three.

- *Link* the new information to what learners already know (south–information). Do this by verbally reminding them of what they know and how it relates to the new information. Or ask for volunteers to explain the connections between the old and new information.

- *Tell* learners where they can go to get more information—other materials, resources, programs, training, and so forth (south–information). Post this information where everyone has access to it.

- *Include* time for learners to paraphrase, in their own words, what they are learning (south–information). Use the Pair Shares, Think and Writes, Pop-Ups, or Doodles in Part One.

- *Direct* learners to work together in cooperative groups for certain activities (west–action). Use the Gallery Walk, Place Your Order, or Metaphor Magic activities in Part One.

- *Follow* a lecture with a practice or review activity that will enable learners to actively use the information (west–action). Use Take a Stand, Blackout Bingo, or Grab That Spoon from Part One, or the "Station Rotation" from Part Three.

- *Include* skills practice, if skill building is part of the training outcome (west–action). Use Each One Teach One from Part One or the "Station Rotation" from Part Three.

- *Give* learners time to create an action plan, that is, a commitment to use the new information after the training is over (west–action). Use Action Plans, Let's Trade, or Tickets Out activities from Part One.

- *Have* learners evaluate their own learning in relation to what they wanted to learn and the WIIFM outcomes (back to north–self). Use the Tickets Out, Walkabout, Blackout Bingo, Early to Finish, Time Sponges, or Celebration activities from Part One.

Besides the activities listed above, the rest of the activities in Part One will also help you include one or more of the four points of the Learning Compass: north–self, east–others, south–information, west–action.

You can use many of the activities for two or more learning steps, depending upon how you structure the activity to fit the purpose of the compass step. For example, use a Pair Share to have learners discuss what they want to learn in the training (north–self), as well as what they already know about the training topic (east–others). Or use a Think and Write when you want learners to review new information (south–information) and to list how many ways they could use the information later (west–action). You might use the Walkabout activity either as an opening (learners discuss what they already know about the topic) or as a closing (learners discuss how they plan to use what they learned). You can use Each One Teach One to review new facts (south–information) or to practice a new skill (west–action).

Compass Questions

Here is another way to make sure you include in your training the four steps in Learning the Natural Way. When designing a learning experience, ask yourself the following questions so that you don't leave out any compass point:

- Have I included time for the north–self step—having learners get in touch with their own learning goals and their own prior knowledge? To do this, choose an activity from the Quick Starts, Connections, or Shout Outs.

- Have I included time for the east–others step—allowing learner-to-learner discussions about what they already know? To do this, choose from the Pair Shares, Postcard Partners, Take a Stand, or Gallery Walk activities.

- Have I linked new knowledge from the south–information step to their previous learning? To do this, choose from the Shout Outs, Think and Writes, or Doodles.

- Have I given them other resources for more learning during the south–information step? Providing both verbal and written resources helps reinforce the learning and reminds learners that they can seek out more information on their own.

- Have I allowed time in the south–information step for them to ask questions and to actively review the new material? To do this, choose from the Think and Writes, Pop-Ups, Shout Outs, Walkabout, and Blackout Bingo activities.

- Have I included an active skills practice or review time in the west–action step? To do this, choose from Each One Teach One, Grab That Spoon, Place Your Order, or the Station Rotation.

- Have I encouraged learners to make action plans and to follow through with them in the west–action step? To do this, choose from the Tickets Out, Early to Finish, Let's Trade, Action Plans, or Walkabout.

Wrapping It Up

When people learn the natural way, they can't help but be successful in the learning experience. Put another way, if your learners are successfully learning what you are teaching them, then you are already using Kolb's natural cycle of learning—whether or not you are aware of it. You are already including the metaphoric Learning Compass with its four steps: north–self, east–others, south–information, west–action.

As we stated at the beginning of this chapter, the most important thing to remember about the Learning Compass is that it is the foundation of the four-step Training Map that is described in the next chapter. Just as a real compass is necessary to create a map of the physical world, the Learning Compass forms the basis of the Training Map. The two tools—compass and map—go hand-in-hand. They are like two sides of the same coin.

Understanding the Learning Compass will deepen your understanding of the Training Map. When you understand how people learn, you can use that knowledge to become better at teaching them in ways that make the learning stick.

The next chapter explains the Training Map and shows you how to use it to transform your training into a more learner-centered, time-efficient experience.

*The trouble with education is that it is too often about teaching
and not enough about learning.*

—Peter Evans

*The business of business is learning.
All else will follow.*

—Harrison Owen

Early to Finish

Pop-Up. Stand up. In your mind, picture a giant directional compass in front of you. Raise your right arm straight up in the air and say, "North–self," as you picture that direction on the compass. Now move your right arm down to shoulder height, hold it out parallel to the ground and say, "East–others." Drop your right arm to your side. Now hold your left arm down in front of you, parallel to your body and say, "South–information." Move your left arm up to shoulder height, parallel to the ground, and say, "West–action." Go through these actions at least two more times, picturing the compass in your mind and following its directional points clockwise, as you state what each point represents. You are grounding the Learning Compass into long-term memory by adding this kinesthetic element to the facts you have already learned in this chapter.

Mapping Your Message

Making It Stick with the Training Map

> ### Quick Start
>
> **Metaphor Magic:** Think about two reasons you might use a road map and write them here:
>
> _____
>
> _____
>
> Now think of the road map as a metaphor for training design. Finish this sentence:
>
> Designing a training is like using a road map because
>
> _____
>
> _____
>
> In this chapter, you'll discover how to use the Training Map, an instructional design tool that will save you both design and delivery time while you progress toward your training destination.

Picture This

You are attending a general automobile maintenance class sponsored by one of the local car dealerships in your city. You arrive and find a seat in the crowded meeting room. You look around to see whether you recognize anyone, but the room is full of strangers. Just then, the dealership owner, Ken, calls for attention, introduces himself to the group, and says, "Car maintenance begins with people caring about their cars and learning from each other how to keep their cars in good working condition. Please take one minute to introduce yourself to the people seated to the left and right of you. Let them know one thing you want to learn here this evening and one thing you already know about good car care." The room fills with noise and energy as everyone begins talking to one another. You feel as though you're with friends now, instead of strangers.

After about sixty seconds, Ken asks for a few volunteers to state what they want to learn and what they already know about car care. Then he explains the goals for the hour-long class.

Ken passes out a note-taking page with pictures of car parts and spaces in which to write. As he lectures, he uses slide photos of car parts projected on a screen. He directs you to write certain words or phrases beside the handout pictures to remind you of each step of car care.

Halfway through the lecture, Ken tells everyone to stand and pair up. Each person must teach his partner one way to take proper care of his car. Partners can correct each other or add to what the other said. When everyone finishes the activity, Ken invites the group into the service area to stand around a car parked there. He directs the group to walk around the car and observe what car care items seem to be missing. When the group returns to the meeting room, Ken leads a whole group discussion about the missing items. Everyone joins the discussion, and the observations include a broken wiper blade, a cracked windshield, worn tires, dirty rearview mirrors, tattered seatbelts, a dangling tailpipe, and the like.

Toward the end of the hour, Ken invites you to tell the people seated to your left and right the three most important things you've learned about car maintenance. After about a minute, he directs you to write on an index card an action plan, that is, one thing you plan to do regularly to take better care of your car. He asks for a few volunteers to state their action plans. He tells you to tape this card to your dashboard so that you will remember to follow through.

Ken summarizes the lecture points and then passes out a schedule of the remaining classes. At the end of the class, he says, "You've made some new friends here tonight—friends who are as interested in keeping their cars in good condition as you are. Please thank them for sharing their time and information with you and give them a round of applause." The room erupts into talking, laughter, and applause. You leave feeling a sense of community with the people around you. You tape your index card to your dashboard as per Ken's instructions. Because of the positive learning experience, you know you will follow through on your action plan. You also know that you will make a point of attending the rest of the car maintenance classes. In fact, you can hardly wait for the next one.

Although you did not realize it at the time, Ken used a four-step Training Map to plan and present his hour-long workshop. He began with having you *make connections* with the other participants and sharing what your goals were, as well as what you already knew about the topic. Then he *explained the concepts* while keeping you engaged with a note-taking activity. After that, he invited you to do a review activity with a partner and then *practice a skill:* checking a car for problems. Finally, you talked about what you had learned, created an action plan on an index card, and *celebrated the learning* by reconnecting once again with your new friends.

Because Ken used this Training Map, you will remember what you learned for a longer period of time. You are also more likely to take better care of your car, and you will definitely sign up for more positive learning experiences like this one.

What Is the Training Map?

Just as we used the metaphor of a directional compass to understand the natural way most people learn, we will use a map metaphor to understand the most effective way to teach others. We'll call this metaphor a Training Map, that is, a format to follow to help us design and deliver more effective learning experiences.

As with a road map that helps you navigate the physical world, the Training Map will help you plan a successful learning journey for your participants. And just as a road map is based on the four coordinates of the directional compass, the Training Map is based on the four steps of the Learning Compass.

The Learning Compass is a metaphor for the four steps of the learning process, and what a learner needs to do in order to remember and use what he learns. The Training Map is a metaphor for the four steps of the teaching process, and what a trainer needs to do in order to make the learning experience meaningful and memorable. The descriptions of both the compass and map may sound similar. Just keep in mind that the compass is a learner's perspective and the map is a trainer's perspective. *Both tools have the same goal: to make the learning stick.*

The person responsible for the practical application and huge success of the Training Map in corporate circles is David Meier, director of the Center for Accelerated Learning. In his book *The Accelerated Learning Handbook* (2000), Meier calls the four-step training model "The Four Phases of Learning." Meier labels each of the four steps as (1) preparation, (2) presentation, (3) practice, and (4) performance.

In this book, we will use a phrase for each of the four steps:

1. Making the connections
2. Explaining the concepts
3. Practicing the skills
4. Celebrating the learning

It doesn't matter what words you use to help you remember the four steps. It just matters that you understand the four-step model and make it your own. You can do this by

- *Choosing* your own metaphor for the training model.
- *Creating* your own titles for each of the four steps.
- *Teaching* the steps to colleagues.
- *Explaining* them to training participants.
- *Making* them work for you and your learners.

Let's explore what you can accomplish by using the Training Map to help you design and deliver learning experiences based on Learning the Natural Way. We will also examine each step in more detail.

What Does a Training Map Do?

When you use the Training Map in your teaching and training, you will

- *Design* learning experiences more easily and in a shorter time.
- *Create* training programs that are based on how people naturally learn, not how they were conditioned to learn.
- *Increase* participants' motivation, interest, and involvement in their own learning.
- *Encourage* training participants to make personal connections to the learning and to the other learners.
- *Link* the new information to what they already know.
- *Give* learners a chance to actively review and apply what they've learned.
- *Enhance* the learners' long-term retention of information.
- *Observe* positive changes in both the cognitive (thinking) and affective (emotional) states of the learners.

- *Use* this powerful model for every presentation or training, regardless of the length of the session, the size or age of your audience, or the topic of your talk.

Using the Training Map

You already use some or all of the four steps of the Training Map. You can't help it. If you're good at what you do, you include these steps because they work, they are based on how people naturally learn, and they are about good teaching. You just may not be consciously aware of the steps, or you might call them by different names. And because you have already read about the Learning Compass, the Training Map will be familiar and easy to understand.

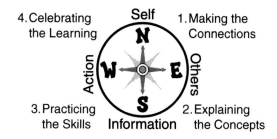

Step One: Making the Connections (from North–Self to East–Others). Meier says that the goal of this first step is "to arouse learners' interest, give them positive feelings about the forthcoming learning experience, and put them into an optimal state for learning" (2000, p. 56). Because you know that learners need to connect with their own learning goals and what they, and others, already know about the training topic, choose opening activities that will give them time to make these connections. When you do this, you also create a psychologically safe learning community, which is a crucial component of successful training. Some of the connecting activities in this book include Quick Starts, Time Sponges, Connections, Pair Shares, Shout Outs, Postcard Partners, the Gallery Walk, and Take a Stand.

Step Two: Explaining the Concepts (from East–Others to South–Information). Meier states that the goal of the second step is "to help the learners encounter the new learning material in ways that are interesting, enjoyable, relevant, and multisensory" (2000, p. 57). *Multisensory* means using the three strongest sensory modalities to help learners absorb new information: auditory (they hear it and talk about it), visual (they see it, draw it, or associate images with it), and kinesthetic (they write it, take notes, associate a movement with it, or stand and move around while learning). Because learners need to link new information to what they already know, give them time to discuss the new material. Divide your lecture time into short segments of ten or twenty minutes. Use a number of the following activities between lecture segments to increase learner involvement and interest: Pair Shares, Shout Outs, Think and Writes, Signals, Doodles, Pop-Ups, and Mark-Ups.

Step Three: Practicing the Skills (from South–Information to West–Action). Meier explains that the goal of the third step is "to help learners integrate and incorporate the new knowledge or skill in a variety of ways" (2000, p. 57). Include time for hands-on practice, building skills, or reviewing what was learned in an active way. Choose from the following activities to help do this: Take a Stand, the Gallery Walk, Grab That Spoon, Place Your Order, Metaphor Magic, Each One Teach One, and Station Rotation.

Step Four: Celebrating the Learning (from West–Action to North–Self). Meier says that the goal of the fourth step is "to help learners apply and extend their new knowledge or skill to the job so that the learning sticks and performance continually improves" (2000, p. 58). In other words, learners need to return to where they first began—to their own learning goals and what they plan to do with what they learned. Build in time during the closing part of your training for them to assess what they learned, make a commitment to use it, and celebrate their learning journey. Choose from the following activities to do this: Tickets Out, Action Plans, Celebrations, Walkabout, and Blackout Bingo.

¡Tips and Variations!

Mess with the Map. You can go back and forth between steps or repeat steps in a training. For example, in a customer service training, you would begin with connecting activities in Step One, and then you might go back and forth between Steps Two and Three as you teach a segment of information and then follow it with an activity, teach another information piece followed by another activity, and so on. So you would teach phone courtesy, followed by a review game. Then you would cover face-to-face service skills followed by partner practice. You would move to online service procedures and follow with computer practice. Finally you would celebrate the learning in Step Four with group projects or skits centered around customer service.

Snip It or Stretch It. You can shorten or lengthen each step, depending upon the total training time you have and what you want to accomplish in that time. For example, if you only have an hour, you might take five minutes to do Step One, thirty minutes for Step Two, fifteen minutes for Step Three, and ten minutes for Step Four (see the Power-Hour Training Templates at the end of this section of the book for more ideas). If you have a day to train, you might spend an hour on Step One, three hours going back and forth between Steps Two and Three, and another hour on Step Four. How you plan your time depends upon the training goals and learning needs of your participants.

Map the Agenda. You can post the map where everyone can see it and use it as an agenda for the training. You can even give learners copies of it to refer to during the training. Even if they aren't familiar with the map, they will catch on quickly as you point out what part of the agenda they are experiencing. And posting it will also keep you on track, tightening up both lecture and activity times.

Assign the Steps. When you do a strong Step One (Making the Connections) at the beginning of the training, participants will be eager to experience Steps Two, Three, and Four. If training time is really short, you can assign some of these steps to be done outside the training room. For example, for Step Two, learners could read topic-related material after the training. For Step Three, they could do real-life skills practice. For Step Four, they could e-mail to you their action plans or evaluation comments about what they learned.

Look for Strengths and Stretches. Be aware of which steps you already do well (your strengths), and which are stretches for you; that is, the steps that you may forget to include or that you don't spend enough time on. For example, you may give an entertaining and informative presentation but forget to follow it with a skills practice. Or you may consistently include the first three steps but always run out of time before celebrating the learning. You might spend the major part of the training on making connections and then scramble to get all the other steps done. Try to include all four steps in your training.

Use Maps Within Maps. You can make a general map overview spanning a week's worth of training and then create smaller, daily maps for each of the five days. All five maps are tied to the training goals and objectives. Or you can create a map overview for a one-day training and then divide it into a "morning map" and an "afternoon map."

Only Map the Important Stuff. Don't go back and redo all your training programs. And for now, don't map every new program you create (unless you're already comfortable using the map). Instead, just modify one or two programs that you think are important enough to justify the time it will take to change them. Or create one map for one new program and run with it first. Begin with baby steps until you're comfortable with this versatile training tool.

Save Yourself Time. The Training Map saves you both design and delivery time. All you have to do is to fill in the concepts to cover and the activities you choose, making sure you have involved your learners during each step. You can quickly see whether you have included the important training pieces, what's missing, and what to add to complete the learning experience. During the training, use it to keep track of where you are, where you're going, and what you need to do in order to get there.

Make It Work for You. The map is a flexible and adaptable tool—you can change it, modify it, tinker with it, mess with it, and use it in unique ways. You can include one, some, or all of the steps. If it makes sense to you and saves you training design and delivery time, then use it. If not, toss it and find something else that works better. As with any tool, the more you use it, the more comfortable you'll be with it.

Make It Work for Your Learners. The map gives you a brain-based structure for designing your training—one that honors the learning needs of your training participants and works because it's how people naturally learn. That said, it *will* work for most of your learners most of the time. Once in awhile, you'll find yourself throwing everything you're doing out the window (including the map) and flying by the seat of your pants. During those times, use your intuition to get you and your learners through. Don't worry about letting go of the agenda and all your wonderfully mapped lesson plans. Just find out what works in that moment and do it. The bottom line? If the map doesn't work for your learners, find something else that does.

Get Started Now. An easy way to begin using the Training Map is to use the Power-Hour Training Templates following this chapter. You'll find five training templates and a template example. The templates show you how to design an hour training by using both the Training Map and many of the activities from Part One. All you have to do is add your own content to the templates to make them work for you.

Wrapping It Up

Because the Training Map is based on Learning the Natural Way, it seems almost elementary: "Of course I use the four-step Training Map. Doesn't everyone?" Unfortunately they don't. Most trainers, having gone through educational systems that used primarily teacher-centered, lecture-based methods of instruction, don't realize that there is a more successful model of teaching and training.

The Training Map is that model. Once you begin to use this tool, you'll never train without it again. It won't make sense to teach in ways other than the natural way people learn. The map will become so second nature to you that you won't even realize you're using it. Both the Learning Compass and Training Map are navigational tools to guide you toward your training goal of making your message stick.

The Power-Hour Training Templates that follow are practical examples of how to use the Training Map and how to include activities from Part One of this book. After you read through the templates, you'll have a clear picture of how to design an hour-long training using what you've learned here. All you need to do is insert your own content pieces into the templates. The templates will help you create learning experiences that are brain-based, motivating, memorable, and completely learner-centered—exactly what you're aiming for.

If you don't know where you're going,
you might end up somewhere else!
—Anonymous

Early to Finish

Read and Think. Look over one of the training agendas or a lesson plan that you have already taught. Can parts of it fit into the steps of the Training Map? Are all four map steps included in the agenda? If not, could you add the steps that are missing, without changing much? If all four steps are present, could you make them stronger or more meaningful for the learners? Can you insert any of the Part One activities into your agenda?

Assessing Your Training Map

The following short assessment will help you determine how complete your Training Map is and which map steps you need to fine-tune in order to finish the map. Rate the following statements as 1 (not yet), 2 (somewhat), or 3 (ready to roll). Your goal is to have 3s (ready to roll) for every statement.

Training Map for [Topic, Title, or Training Event]
Step One: Making the Connections

_____ The opening begins with a short activity that connects learners to the topic (what learners already know and what they want to learn), to each other, and to you, the training instructor (examples: Quick Starts, Connections).

_____ The opening is interesting enough to catch the learners' attention.

_____ The opening statements include the training goals and objectives.

Step Two: Explaining the Concepts

_____ The concepts are divided into short lecture segments of about ten minutes in length.

_____ The lecture segments include visual aids (examples: graphics, cartoons, doodles, job aids or job-related objects, personal stories that create mental pictures, or real-life vignettes).

_____ Each lecture segment is followed by a short (one-minute) review activity to involve learners and help them remember the concepts (examples: Shout Outs, Pair Shares, Think and Write, Doodles, Signals, Mark-Ups, Pop-Ups).

Step Three: Practicing the Skills

_____ The training contains a short review activity or game (examples: Grab That Spoon, Gallery Walk, Place Your Order), or time for a group discussion in which learners talk about how they can use what they learned.

_____ If there are skills included in the training, learners have time to practice a skill in pairs or small groups (examples: Each One Teach One, "Station Rotation").

Step Four: Celebrating the Learning

_____ The closing contains a short summary of the most important concepts.

_____ During the closing, learners make an action plan, that is, a written or verbal statement about how they plan to use what they learned (examples: Tickets Out, Action Plans).

_____ The closing contains a short activity that ends the training on a high-energy note (example: Celebrations).

Power-Hour Training Templates

Time-Saving Design and Delivery Tools

Quick Start

Fill in the missing words:

1. A _____ is to a cook as a blueprint is to _____.

2. A pattern is to _____ as a _____ is to a mechanic.

3. A layout is to _____ as a _____ is to a movie.

4. A _____ is to a pilot as a template is to _____.

Check your answers (your answers are correct if they make sense contextually, even if they aren't the same words as the ones below):

1. recipe, an architect

2. a tailor, manual

3. a Web site, storyboard

4. flight plan, a trainer

By now, you're convinced that chunking your material into 10-minute segments is probably a good thing. You agree that involving learners in short, quick activities between the ten-minute lecture segments will help them remember the information longer. You know how important it is to have a safe learning community. You want to use the Training Map so that participants can learn the natural way. You realize that if you want learners to apply the new information to their own jobs and lives, they need time to discuss what they plan to do with what they learned. In fact, you wholeheartedly agree with the two major concepts of this book: *shorter segments of instruction are better than longer ones, and learners remember more when they are involved in the learning.*

The question remains: How do you use all the concepts you've learned in this book when you only have an hour of training time? The answer is easy: you use a Power-Hour Training Template, which will save you both design and delivery time.

Why a Power-Hour Training Template?

We use templates for a lot of activities: designing a Web site (think *layout*), cooking (think *recipe*), building a house (*blueprint*), sewing (*pattern*)—in fact, most of what we do as humans begins with mental images or templates, which are formats, patterns, or sequences we'll use to help us do what we want to do.

That's the point: *Templates simply help us do what we want or need to do—and they save us time.* Lots of time. We use templates when we want to speed up the creating or doing of something.

The Power-Hour Training Templates are training design formats already created and ready to use. They won't show you what to teach—you are the expert when it comes to your topics and material. Instead, they will show you how to put together an hour of training by using your material and the ideas and activities from *The Ten-Minute Trainer.*

If you are already quick at training design, or if you can take one idea and instantly see six ways to use it, you probably don't need these training templates. *But if you're short on time and would like a design "jump start," these templates will serve that purpose.*

What a Power-Hour Template Can Do

Besides reducing the time it will take you to design an hour of training, when you use these training templates you will

- *Get* a hands-on feel for how the activities in this book can be inserted into your training content.
- *Practice* the concepts you've learned from this book.

- *Apply* these new ideas and activities to a variety of training topics.
- *Feel* more comfortable with what you have learned.
- *Increase* learner involvement and retention of the material you teach.
- *Become* a more time-efficient training professional.

The first three training templates will show you how to organize a training hour with ten-minute lecture segments. The fourth and fifth templates will give you examples of a training hour with fifteen- and twenty-minute lecture segments. In all five templates, you insert your own training material into the lecture segments. The five training templates are followed by one example of how to use a template with actual training content.

¡Tips and Variations!

Make It Longer or Shorter. If you have less than an hour to train, shorten the template. If you have more than an hour to train, lengthen the template or combine two or more templates.

Chunk Your Stuff. Before you train, divide your lecture material into ten-minute segments. For an hour, you'll need four or five segments, since you'll also be including sixty-second activities or a five- or ten-minute game.

Close Enough Is OK. If you're not used to lecturing for only ten minutes at a time, aim for fifteen or twenty minutes to begin with. Instead of using the first three templates, which divide your material into ten-minute segments, use the last two templates, which divide your material into fifteen- and twenty-minute segments.

Use the Need-to-Know Rule. If you have difficulty editing your material so that it fits shorter instructional segments, use the need-to-know rule: *Only include what learners need to know about the topic in your lecture, such as the crucial concepts, the most important facts, the how-to-apply-it suggestions.* Any other nice-to-know information can go on written handouts for training participants to read later.

Teach to the Take-Aways. Before you train, decide on the specific take-aways— outcomes or behaviors—you want your learners to walk away with by the end of the training. Make sure you tie each of your lecture segments—and the activities—to these outcomes.

A Picture's Worth a Thousand Words. Whenever possible, use images to enhance your lecture segments—visuals, graphics, cartoons, icons, photos, drawings, symbols, stories, metaphors, and analogies. If using computer slides, make sure they contain clip art, too, and that they aren't just the printed words of what you're saying. Remember: learners can include doodles in their note taking, as well as words.

Have It Handy. Put the materials that learners will need within their reach so you don't waste training time passing these things out. Materials may include: handouts, scratch paper, chart paper, index cards, pens or pencils, felt pens, Post-it® notes, etc.

Slanted Words Are Yours. All the activities in the templates that are from Part One of this book are numbered according to their numerical order in that particular Part One section. For example, if a template activity is titled "Pair Share #5," it means that it is the fifth Pair Share in the Pair Shares section. In the templates, the italicized sentences after the activity titles are what you say to the learners. Of course, these sentences are suggestions only—change them as you wish.

They're Mapped for You. Since the blueprint for the templates is the Training Map, read the Learning Compass and Training Map sections of Part Two before you choose one of these templates to use (Let the Compass Be Your Guide, and Mapping Your Message, respectively). After reading those sections, the template design will make more sense to you.

Tinker with the Template. Make the templates work for you and your learners. They are meant to be guides only, so feel free to experiment, change, and adapt them to the learning needs of all.

Let It Go. Nothing works all the time. If you find yourself struggling with a template, and it is costing you training design or delivery time, let it go. It's meant to be a time-saving, useful tool—nothing more.

Wrapping It Up

The Power-Hour Training Templates will help you become comfortable with the concepts and activities in *The Ten-Minute Trainer*. They will also save you design time while you become proficient at using these new training tools. Once you do that, you'll be creating your own training templates in no time.

The only reason for time is so that
everything doesn't happen at once.

—Albert Einstein

Early to Finish

Read and Think. Skip to the Power-Hour Template Sample and read it first so that you get an idea of how you might use the templates. Then read the templates and begin thinking about how you could use them in your own training.

Power-Hour Training Template #1

With Five 10-Minute Lecture Segments

Training Title:

Training Duration:

Group Size:

Need to Knows (Major Concepts):

Take-Aways (Outcomes to Expect):

Setup, Materials, Reminders:

- Post the Quick Start where everyone can see it (chart, overhead, slide).

- Materials: handouts, index cards, pens or pencils, small noisemakers (whistles, clappers, or the like)—one of each item per person.

- Pass out all materials before the training begins, or place them on tables within reach of the participants.

Notes:

Training Map

Step One: Making the Connections

Learning Compass
From North–Self to East–Others

1 minute	Quick Start #1: Post the following where everyone can read it: *After reading this, introduce yourself to someone you don't know and ask that person to list three things he hopes to learn from this training.* Begin by directing participants to read and do the Quick Start.
2 minutes	Introduction and Opening Statements

Training Map

Step Two: Explaining the Concepts

Learning Compass
From East–Others to South–Information

10 minutes	Lecture Segment #1
1 minute	Pair Share #1: *Turn to your neighbor—the person sitting next to you (please make sure no one is left out)—and tell him the most important fact you just learned in the last ten minutes.*
10 minutes	Lecture Segment #2
1 minute	Think and Write #1: *Think about the material we've just covered. On one side of an index card, write one sentence that summarizes this information.*
10 minutes	Lecture Segment #3
1 minute	Pop-Up #10: *Stand up and ask the person standing next to you a question about the material we've covered (make sure no one is left out). Give her a "thumbs up" if she answers the question to your satisfaction. Sit down when you are done.*
10 minutes	Lecture Segment #4

Training Map

Step Three: Practicing the Skills

Learning Compass
From South–Information to West–Action

1 minute	Shout Out #4: *Shout out four ways you can use the information we've covered so far.*
10 minutes	Lecture Segment #5 (include other ways to apply the information)

Training Map

Step Four: Celebrating the Learning

Learning Compass
From West–Action to North–Self

1 minute	Summary and Closing Statements (include "next steps" and resources for more information)
1 minute	Action Plan #4: *On the back of your index card, jot down two things you are going to do with this new information. Now compare your card with a neighbor's to see whether your action plans are the same or different.*
1 minute	Celebration #3: Announce that the noisemakers are training souvenirs and direct participants to each take one. Say, *Sound your noisemaker if you learned at least four things that you didn't know before. Make a noise if you can use what you've learned in this past hour. Sound your noisemaker if you had fun while learning.*

Power-Hour Training Template #2

With Four 10-Minute
and One 5-Minute Lecture Segments

Training Title:

Training Duration:

Group Size:

Need to Knows (Major Concepts):

Take-Aways (Outcomes to Expect):

Setup, Materials, Reminders:

- Post the Quick Start where everyone can see it (chart, overhead, slide).

- Materials: handouts, index cards (two per person), plastic spoons (one for every four to six people), small bag or box by the door.

- Pass out all materials before the training begins, or have them on tables and within reach of the participants. You can also put them in the bag or box by the door and direct participants to take one of each as they walk in.

- Make up an oral question about the material you cover in Lecture Segment #2. Be ready to state the question after the lecture.

- Before the training, read the Grab That Spoon game instructions in the "Take Five!" section of Part One. Become familiar enough with the instructions so that you can quickly tell learners how to play the game.

Notes:

Training Map

Step One: Making the Connections

Learning Compass
From North–Self to East–Others

1 minute	Quick Start #3: Post the following where everyone can read it: *After reading this, stand and take a short "survey" by asking three other participants what they want to learn today. Be ready to state your "survey" results when asked to do so.* Begin by directing participants to do the Quick Start.
1 minute	Processing the Quick Start: Ask for a few volunteers to state what their survey results were.
2 minutes	Introduction and Opening Statements

Training Map

Step Two: Explaining the Concepts

Learning Compass
From East–Others to South–Information

10 minutes	Lecture Segment #1
1 minute	Mark-Up #7: Direct learners to a handout page that contains information related to the material you just covered in your lecture. Say: *Quickly read the bulleted items on this page of the handout. Circle the three that are the most important (the most meaningful, the most useful) to you.*
10 minutes	Lecture Segment #2
1 minute	Signal #6: *I am going to ask you a question about the material we've covered. Stand if you're pretty sure you can answer the question correctly. Remain seated if you're not sure, or if you want more time to think about it.* State your question and wait until some participants stand up. Then say: *Standing people, please share your answer with the seated people. When you are done, you can sit back down.*

10 minutes	Lecture Segment #3
1 minute	Think and Write #8: *On an index card, write down a test question related to this material. Write the answer to the question on the back of the card. Give the card a point value from 1 to 10 (1 = an easy question, 10 = a hard question). Hold onto the card for a quick game later.*
10 minutes	Lecture Segment #4

Training Map

Step Three: Practicing the Skills

Learning Compass
From South–Information to West–Action

5 minutes	Grab That Spoon Game: Follow the game instructions from the "Take Five!" section of Part One. Have learners use the question cards they made earlier in the training. Applaud the winners in each group. If time allows, ask some of the processing questions included in the game instructions.
5 minutes	Lecture Segment #5 (include ways to apply the information)

Training Map

Step Four: Celebrating the Learning

Learning Compass
From West–Action to North–Self

1 minute	Action Plan #2: *Tell two people seated close to you two things you plan to do with what you've learned in this hour.*
1 minute	Summary and Closing Statement (include "next steps" and resources for more information)
1 minute	Celebration #7: *Look at the folks around you and, on the count of three, shout with me, "Good going, gang!"* (You can choose a different phrase for everyone to shout.) End with a round of applause for all.

Power-Hour Training Template #3

With Four 10-Minute
and One 5-Minute Lecture Segments

Training Title:

Training Duration:

Group Size:

Need to Knows (Major Concepts):

Take-Aways (Outcomes to Expect):

Setup, Materials, Reminders:

- Make up a question related to the material in Lecture Segment #1. Print the question on a chart, overhead, or slide, and have it ready to show learners after the lecture.

- Make up some true-or-false statements about the material in Lecture Segment #3. Be ready to use them after the lecture.

- Materials: handouts, pens or pencils, souvenirs (small, penny items—one per person), small bag or box.

- Have all materials except for the souvenirs within reach of the participants. Put the souvenirs in a small bag or box to pass out at the end of the hour.

- Before the training, read the Each One Teach One activity instructions in the "Take Five!" section of Part One. Become comfortable enough with the activity instructions that you can quickly explain them to the learners.

Notes:

Training Map

Step One: Making the Connections

Learning Compass
From North–Self to East–Others

1 minute	Connection #1: Begin the training by saying: *Quickly introduce yourself to someone seated near you (make sure that no one around you is left out) and tell your new friend two things: what you want to learn today and one fact you already know about the training topic.*
2 minutes	Introduction and Opening Statements

Training Map

Step Two: Explaining the Concepts

Learning Compass
From East–Others to South–Information

10 minutes	Lecture Segment #1
1 minute	Pop-Up #1: Post the lecture-related question where everyone can see it and say: *The last person in your table group (or row) to pop out of his chair answers this question for your group. Your group will let him know if his answer is correct by giving him a round of applause.*
10 minutes	Lecture Segment #2
1 minute	Doodle #1: *On your handout, draw a doodle representing the most important thing you've just learned. Your doodle can be a line, a shape, a squiggle, an icon, a cartoon, anything visual. Explain your doodle to the person sitting next to you.*
10 minutes	Lecture Segment #3
1 minute	Signal #3: *When I make a statement related to the information we just covered, clap your hands if you agree with the statement or stomp your*

feet if you don't agree. Read your true-false statements, waiting for learners to either clap or stomp after each statement.

10 minutes   Lecture Segment #4

Training Map

Step Three: Practicing the Skills

Learning Compass
From South–Information to West–Action

5 minutes   Each One Teach One Activity: Follow the activity instructions from the "Take Five!" section of Part One. End the activity with applause for everyone.

5 minutes   Lecture Segment #5 (include other ways to apply the information)

Training Map

Step Four: Celebrating the Learning

Learning Compass
From West–Action to North–Self

2 minutes   Summary and Closing Statements (include "next steps" and resources for more information)

1 minute   Celebration #10: Pass out individual training souvenirs. Say: *Hold up your souvenir. This is to remind you that you make a difference in the lives of those you live with and work with. It's also a reminder of what you learned today. As you hold up this souvenir, give the folks around you a high-five.* Then end with a round of applause for all.

1 minute   Ticket Out #7: Stand by the door and say: *As you leave, please tell me one idea you plan to put to use after this training is over.*

Power-Hour Training Template #4
With Three 15-Minute Lecture Segments

Training Title:

Training Duration:

Group Size:

Need to Knows (Major Concepts):

Take-Aways (Outcomes to Expect):

Setup, Materials, Reminders:

- Materials: handouts, pens or pencils, postcard pieces (see below), index cards, Post-it® notes—one of each item per person.

- Make sure all materials are within reach of the participants.

- Before the training, read the Postcard Partners and Walkabout instructions for both activities in the "Take Five!" section of Part One. Become comfortable enough with the instructions that you can quickly explain them to the learners.

- Before the training, prepare the postcard pieces as per the activity instructions. Make sure you have enough pieces—one for each participant.

Notes:

Training Map

Step One: Making the Connections

Learning Compass
From North–Self to East–Others

5 minutes	Postcard Partners Activity: Follow the activity instructions from the "Take Five!" section of Part One. Direct learners to give their postcard partners a high-five at the end of the activity.
1 minute	Introduction and Opening Statements

Training Map

Step Two: Explaining the Concepts

Learning Compass
From East–Others to South–Information

15 minutes	Lecture Segment #1
1 minute	Doodle #7: *On an index card, write down the three most important concepts we've talked about so far. Beside each concept, draw an image, a doodle, or a shape to represent it. If you have time, share your index card with your neighbor.*
15 minutes	Lecture Segment #2
1 minute	Mark-Up #6: *In the margin of your handout, write a one-sentence reaction to this information (or your opinion about the material, or one question, comment, or concern).*
15 minutes	Lecture Segment #3

Training Map

Step Three: Practicing the Skills

Learning Compass
From South–Information to West–Action

5 minutes   The Walkabout Activity: Follow the activity instructions from the "Take Five!" section of Part One. Direct learners to pair up with their Postcard Partners for the Walkabout. Suggest that they talk about how they plan to use what they've learned.

Training Map

Step Four: Celebrating the Learning

Learning Compass
From West–Action to North–Self

1 minute   Summary and Closing Statements (include "next steps" and resources for more information)

1 minute   Celebration #5: *On a Post-it® note, write a thank-you or compliment for your Postcard Partner. Stick the Post-it® to your partner's arm (or hand it to him) as you walk out the door.*

Power-Hour Training Template #5

With Two 20-Minute
and One 5-Minute Lecture Segments

Training Title:

Training Duration:

Group Size:

Need to Knows (Major Concepts):

Take-Aways (Outcomes to Expect):

Setup, Materials, Reminders:

- Before the training, read the Gallery Walk activity instructions in the "Take Five!" section of Part One. Become comfortable enough with the activity instructions that you can quickly explain them to the learners.

- Before the training, make and hang the wall charts according to the Gallery Walk instructions.

- Materials: handouts, pens or pencils, broad-tipped colored felt pens (for the Gallery Walk)—one of each item per person.

- Make sure all materials are within reach of the participants.

Notes:

Training Map

Step One: Making the Connections

Learning Compass
From North–Self to East–Others

5 minutes	The Gallery Walk Activity: Follow the activity instructions from the "Take Five!" section of Part One. Do just the writing part of the activity during this time. At the end of five minutes, let the participants know that they will have time to read the gallery charts toward the end of the hour.
1 minute	Introduction and Opening Statements

Training Map

Step Two: Explaining the Concepts

Learning Compass
From East–Others to South–Information

20 minutes	Lecture Segment #1
1 minute	Pair Share #4: *Make up a quick question about what you've just learned. Ask the person sitting next to you the question (make sure no one around you is left out). If that person answers correctly, give him a thumbs-up.*
20 minutes	Lecture Segment #2
1 minute	Mark-Up #5: Direct participants to a handout page related to the material you just covered. Say: *Underline (or highlight) the main ideas (or most meaningful words or phrases) on this page.*

Training Map

Step Three: Practicing the Skills

Learning Compass
From South–Information to West–Action

5 minutes	The Gallery Walk Activity Revisited: Follow the activity instructions from the "Take Five!" section of Part One. For about three minutes, participants will walk around and read the wall charts. Then you lead a two-minute, whole group discussion about what learners observed and learned from the activity.
5 minutes	Lecture Segment #3 (include ways to apply the information)

Training Map

Step Four: Celebrating the Learning

Learning Compass
From West–Action to North–Self

1 minute	Summary and Closing Statements (include "next steps" and resources for more information)
1 minute	Action Plan #9: *Think of two things you plan to do with this new information and one person at work you could share this information with. Tell a person near you what you thought of.* End with a round of applause for all.

Power-Hour Training Sample

Using Template #1:
Five 10-Minute Lecture Segments

Training Title: I See What You Say! An Introduction to Communication Styles.

Training Duration: 60 minutes.

Group Size: Any size is fine.

Need to Knows (Major Concepts):
- There are four major communication styles.
- Each style has its own communication needs.
- Once you understand what each style needs, you can "style-stretch" to meet those communication needs.
- Style-stretching means giving others what they need and asking for what you need.

Take-Aways (Outcomes to Expect):
- Learners will be able to define the four communication styles and the communication needs of each style.
- Learners will be able to explain their own communication "strengths" and "stretches."
- Learners will decide what they will do in their own lives with this new information.
- Learners will make a commitment to apply one of the communication strategies during an interaction with a coworker, a family member, or a friend.

Setup, Materials, Reminders:

- Post the Quick Start where everyone can see it (chart, overhead, slide).
- Materials: handouts, index cards, pens or pencils, small noisemakers (whistles, clappers, or the like)—one of each item per person.
- Cartoons for Lecture Segments #1, #2.
- Handouts: three pages (Communication Styles Descriptions, Style-Stretching, Communication Challenge and Style-Stretching Solution).
- Charts or overhead transparencies to write on; felt pens or transparency pens.
- Pass out all materials before the training begins, or place them on tables within reach of the participants.

Notes:

Training Map

Step One: Making the Connections

Learning Compass
From North–Self to East–Others

1 minute   Quick-Start #1: Post the following where everyone can read it: *After reading this, introduce yourself to someone you don't know and ask that person to list three things about communication that he wants to learn in this session.* Say: *Take sixty seconds to read and do the Quick Start posted here.*

2 minutes   Introduction and Opening Statements: Say: *Let's hear five things you want to learn in this hour on communication.* Elicit five verbal responses. Then say, *In addition to what you want to learn, you will also walk out with these take-aways: First, you will be able to define the four communication styles and their communication needs. Second, you will be able to explain your own communication style strengths and stretches. Third, you will decide what you plan to do with this information in your own personal or professional life. Fourth, you'll make a commitment to try a new communication strategy and see how it works.* Direct learners to think about what they already know about communication styles. Explain that they are going to link some new information to what they already know. Emphasize that there are about thirty to forty existing styles-based programs, each with its own twist on diversity: communication styles, personality styles, management or leadership styles, conflict-resolution styles, and so forth. All these programs are based on the same research and all are different ways of looking at why we do what we do.

Training Map

Step Two: Explaining the Concepts

Learning Compass
From East–Others to South–Information

10 minutes   Lecture Segment #1: Using cartoons representing each communication style, explain that there are four major communication styles, which are four general ways of communicating that are easily recognizable. Each style is represented by the following four names, which stand for that style's particular communication needs:

1. Peacemakers. Need a feeling of personal rapport and emotional acceptance in order to communicate effectively.

2. Truthkeepers. Need to know that what is being communicated is logical, accurate, and fits with what they know.

3. Solutionseekers. Need to know what the bottom line is and how they can use what is being discussed.

4. Risktakers. Need a feeling of excitement, discovery, and a sharing of energy in order to communicate effectively.

Have the learners repeat aloud the names of the styles with you. Give a few verbal examples of what a person with each style preference might say when talking to someone. Then have learners turn to the handout page labeled "Communication Style Descriptions" and silently skim the style lists, checking any item that describes their own preferred style. Explain that they will begin to notice patterns: maybe their preference is one style over the others or two styles, or maybe only one style is weak and the others are pretty balanced.

1 minute   Pair Share #1: *Turn to your neighbor—the person sitting next to you (please make sure no one is left out)—and tell him the most important fact that you just learned about communication or about your own preferred communication style in the last ten minutes.*

10 minutes	Lecture Segment #2: Show a cartoon of a person physically stretching to reach another person, which is labeled "Style-Stretching: Giving others what they need and asking for what I need." Explain that style-stretching simply means giving other people what they need when communicating. It also means asking for what you need so that the other person doesn't have to guess. Have learners say with you: *Style-Stretching: Giving others what they need and asking for what I need.* Give examples of style-stretching with short vignettes. Or elicit one or two verbal examples from the learners.
1 minute	Think and Write #1: *Think about the material we've just covered. On one side of an index card, write one sentence that summarizes this information. On the other side of the card, write down what you think your own communication style strengths and stretches are. If you have time, share one strength or stretch with the person sitting next to you.*
10 minutes	Lecture Segment #3: Ask for two volunteers to verbally share their own communication strengths and stretches with the group. Explain that the Golden Rule doesn't work when it comes to communication (that is, "Do unto others as you wish them to do unto you"). Instead, the Platinum Rule needs to be followed: "Do unto others as they wish to be done unto." This is where style-stretching comes into play. Direct learners to take notes on the handout packet "Style-Stretching" page while you lecture and write these items:

1. With Peacemakers: Small talk first; ask about them; suggest—don't tell; give them time to see how they feel about it; show them acceptance and that you value who they are.

2. With Truthkeepers: Written plan; accurate details; be logical; downplay emotions; cite your sources; ask what they know; give them time to think about it; show that you value their expertise.

3. With Solutionseekers: The bottom line first; emphasize the practicality and usefulness; skip the details; ask for their solutions; show that you value their willingness to act on the information.

4. With Risktakers: Energy first; keep it alive and exciting; leave out details and explore possibilities; emphasize the challenge; talk about the big picture; show that you value their vision.

Ask the learners what else they can add to the "Style-Stretching" lists. Add their suggestions to your written lists and direct them to write their own suggestions on their note-taking pages.

1 minute	Pop-Up #10: *Stand up and ask the person standing next to you a question about the style-stretching material we've covered (make sure no one is left out). Give her a thumbs-up if she answers the question to your satisfaction. Sit down when you are done.*
10 minutes	Lecture Segment #4: Give a few practical examples in story-format of ways to style-stretch both at work and at home to meet the needs of the four communication styles. Use personal vignettes. Make the stories as concrete as possible so that learners begin to see how to apply the style-stretching strategies in real-life situations. Ask for a volunteer or two to share a real-life example as well.

Training Map

Step Three: Practicing the Skills

Learning Compass
From South–Information to West–Action

1 minute	Shout Out #4: *Shout out four ways you can use the information we've covered so far.*
10 minutes	Lecture Segment #5: Direct learners to turn to the handout page labeled "Communication Challenge and Style-Stretching Solution." Give them a minute to jot down a real-life communication challenge they have experienced. They also write what style-stretching strategies they could use to meet the challenge. Explain that nothing works all the time but that style-stretching can sometimes save the day—*and* the relationship. Emphasize the value of trying out new ways of communicating, especially with those

who matter the most in their lives. Also remind them that the definition of insanity is doing the same thing over and over but expecting different results. If what they are doing in communicating isn't working, they need to try something else. If time allows, ask for a volunteer to share what he or she wrote on the "Communication Challenge" page.

Training Map

Step Four: Celebrating the Learning

Learning Compass
From West–Action to North–Self

1 minute	Summary and Closing Statements: Say: *You can now state what the four general communication styles are and explain their communication needs. You've taken a look at your own communication style preferences, and how to stretch to another style to make the communication work. You've also applied style-stretching strategies to a real-life situation. Here is where you can get more information on this topic.* (Tell them about any resources—books, Web sites, and so forth.)
1 minute	Action Plan #4: *On the back of your handout, jot down two things you are going to do with this new information. Now compare what you wrote with a neighbor's response to see whether your action plans are the same or different.*
1 minute	Celebration #3: Announce that the noisemakers are training souvenirs and direct participants to each take one. Say: *Sound your noisemaker if you learned at least four things about communication that you didn't know before. Make a noise if you can use what you've learned in this past hour. Sound your noisemaker if you had fun while learning about communication styles.*

Note: This sample is from Sharon Bowman's manual *Effective Communication Skills Training* and is reprinted with permission of Pfeiffer for *The Ten-Minute Trainer.* Please cite the source when using the content of this sample.

Part Three

More Timely Training Tools

Quick Start

Mark-Up: Check off all the concepts below that *The Ten-Minute Trainer* has covered in depth so far:

Sixty-Second Activities	CLUE Elements	The Learning Compass
Training Templates	Got a Minute?	Five- and Ten-Minute Games
Attention Maker	Check for Understanding	
Station Rotation	Three Brains in One	The Training Map
Imagery in Learning	Television's Role	Attention Breaker
Power-Hour Training Templates	Four Levels of Training Competence	The RAS

You probably checked all but the following concepts:

CLUE Elements	Check for Understanding	Station Rotation
Imagery in Learning	Four Levels of Training Competence	

Part Three covers these concepts in detail. As you read this part of the book, you may be familiar with some of these ideas because they are variations of what you have already learned. When you review old material in new ways, you will discover other uses for it that may not have occurred to you at first.

According to William Howell, as quoted by Robert Pike in *Creative Training Techniques Handbook,* there are four basic levels of training competence. As you read the bulleted points, do what the first sentence of each paragraph describes:

• *Put your hands on your hips and say, "I don't know that I don't know."* Howell calls it "unconscious incompetence." At this level, we are so new to the training profession that we don't have a clue as to what we really know or don't know. In fact, we may think we are quite good at training—until we stand in front of a roomful of participants all looking expectantly at us, and we suddenly realize how much we don't know.

• *Put your hands on your shoulders and say, "I know that I don't know."* Howell says this is "conscious incompetence." At this level, we know how much more we still need to learn. We actively seek out learning experiences that will teach us what we need to know. We may attend train-the-trainer workshops, read training books, or study under a master trainer.

• *Put your hands on your head and say, "I know that I know."* Howell calls this "conscious competence." At this level, we are confident in our abilities to design and deliver effective training. We've had the education and experience we need to be really good at what we do. Best of all, when asked, we can explain to our colleagues the *what, why,* and *how* of what we do, and show them how to do it too.

• *Put your hands in the air over your head and say, "I don't know that I know."* Howell labels this "unconscious competence." At this level, we are so good at what we do, and have done it well for so long, that it's second nature to us. Like a life-long physical skill, this stage of competence is almost cellular, a "muscle-knowing" of the mind. When asked how we got to be such excellent trainers, we just smile and say, "I don't know how I learned all this. I don't even know how it really works. I just know that it works for me and for my learners."

Now quickly repeat aloud the four bold print sentences while putting your hands on your hips, shoulders, head, and overhead:

• **I don't know that I don't know.**

• **I know that I don't know.**

• **I know that I know.**

• **I don't know that I know.**

See whether you can do it one more time without looking at the sentences— just by remembering them from your hand motions.

Why the hand motions and association of body parts? Because linking pieces of information to parts of the body will help you remember the information longer. And if you verbally and kinesthetically repeat this procedure at least six times throughout the day, you will move it into long-term memory where you can access it days or weeks from now.

Bringing It Home to Conscious Competence

In reading *The Ten-Minute Trainer,* if you have moved from the second to the third level of training competence, you now have new information to consider when designing and delivering effective training. You have new activities to experiment with and new concepts to explore. You're eager to try these new training tools.

If you have moved from the fourth to the third level of training competence, you already knew much of the information in this book and just needed to be reminded that you knew it. As you read *The Ten-Minute Trainer,* you probably thought, "Of course, I already knew that," or "I do that all the time."

Either way, your goal in reading this book has been to achieve conscious competence, the level at which you are not only skilled at designing and delivering effective training but can also explain what you are doing, why it works, and how others can do it as well as you do.

You've arrived at the conscious competence level when you have

- *Polished* your training programs by including ideas and activities from Part One
- *Applied* the research and training design tools from Part Two to make your training work even better for you and your learners
- *Created* new learning experiences and fine-tuned existing ones by using some of the concepts from Part Three

More Tools for the Consciously Competent Trainer

Part Three includes more tools for you, the consciously competent trainer. As you combine your own artistry as a trainer (the affective or feeling part of what you do) with the science of effective teaching and learning (the brain research and cognitive part of what you do), you will take these extra tools, tinker with them, and change them to make them your own.

With "Get a CLUE!" you'll discover four elements necessary for motivation and memory in learning. You already use some, if not all, of these elements. Consciously including all four dramatically increases learners' interest in the material and their retention of important information.

In "What's a Picture Worth?" you'll be reminded of the power of the image in training. You already know that television-saturated cultures rely heavily on images for education as well as entertainment. In this chapter, you'll find out how to make your training image-rich.

"You Said It But Did They Get It?" offers you five ways to check for understanding so that you know whether your training participants are learning and remembering the new information. Some of these methods have also been described in Part One. Here they are used as assessment tools.

The "Station Rotation" is a unique, highly active, fast-paced learning activity. You can use it to introduce new material, review what has been already covered, apply the learned content in various ways, or do all three at the same time. It is versatile enough to use in a number of different ways to increase motivation and memory.

Wrapping It Up

These training tools are timely because you are now ready to add them to your growing list of effective training methods. As a consciously competent trainer, you'll fine-tune them so that they save you time in both designing and delivering quality programs. They are reminders of what you already know, of what you have learned, and of what you can do to make your training even better.

You don't understand anything
until you learn it in more than one way.
—Marvin Minsky

Early to Finish

Each One Teach One. If you have a few extra minutes and also have a family member, friend, or colleague close at hand, teach this person the Four Levels of Training Competence, including the motions that go with the concepts. You will remember them longer because you taught them to someone else.

Author Richard Bach said it best: "We master what we teach."

Anytime you want to remember something, teach it to another person. Anytime you want to truly understand something, teach it to someone else. And anytime you want your learners to remember what they learned in your training, have them teach it to each other—and to colleagues, friends, and their own family members.

Get a CLUE!

Four Elements to Increase Motivation and Memory in Learning

It's no secret that classrooms and training rooms often house reluctant, resistant learners. Some folks just don't want to be there—and with good reason. Maybe the class is mandatory but irrelevant, unrelated to what the learners' interests are or what they do. Maybe the course content, or the teaching methods, are just plain boring.

It's also common knowledge that teachers and trainers are expected to motivate these reluctant learners. Even knowing that motivation is an intrinsic thing—it has to come from within the learner himself—the expectation is unspoken but clear:

Thou shalt motivate others to learn.

This is the expectation, in spite of the fact that humans are motivated to learn what interests *them,* not what interests the teacher or the company. The human brain resists learning information that it does not consider important.

As trainers, we can indirectly affect a person's motivation to learn through the training methods we choose. We can help learners motivate themselves when we make a training interesting and relevant. To do that, we have four motivational tools available to us that will increase the probability that learners will not only want to learn but will also use what they learn once the training is over.

What Are the Four CLUE Elements?

According to educational research, there are four crucial elements that increase both motivation and memory in learning. Including all four elements in a training program ensures that learners will remain interested and involved the entire time and that they will be able to remember what they learn and use it in their work or life.

The letters in the acronym CLUE stand for these four elements. The acronym will help you remember how to make your training both motivational and memorable.

The four elements are

C = Creative

L = Linked

U = Useful

E = Emotional

Creative means you consistently choose methods of teaching and learning that are interesting, unusual, and intriguing to the participants. You not only exercise your own creativity in designing and delivering unforgettable training, but you also allow time for learners to practice and apply the new information in creative ways. Creativity always engages both the curiosity and interest of the learner, as well as right-brain thinking skills (see "Attention Maker, Attention Breaker" in Part Two for more information on holding the learner's interest, and "What's a Picture Worth?" in Part Three for more on the right and left hemispheres of the thinking brain).

Linked means that you provide ample opportunities for learners to link the training concepts to what they already know, that is, to link the new to the old.

When learners have time to do this, they deepen their own understanding of the material and can remember it longer.

Useful means that the new information is directly applicable to learners' lives. Participants see how they can put the new concepts to use in practical ways to make their work or lives even better.

Emotional means that there is a positive correlation between what training participants are learning and how they feel about what they are learning. Since emotion directs attention, which directs learning, it is really important to make the learning experience a positive one (see "Three Brains in One" in Part Two for more on the importance of emotions in learning).

What Does CLUE Do?

When you include the four CLUE elements—creative, linked, useful, emotional—in your training, learners will

- *Engage* in the learning in interactive and productive ways.
- *Focus* on what they are learning and how they can use it in their own lives.
- *Create* their own learning methods and applications.
- *Show* enthusiasm about and interest in what they are learning.
- *Ask* and answer their own questions.
- *Discuss* and debate concepts.
- *Analyze* the new material to see what fits with what they know and can do.
- *Decide* how they will use what they are learning.
- *Synthesize* the new material to see what other uses they can find for it.
- *Ask* for more of the same kind of learning experience.

The Creative Element

To make your training more creative, add the following to the training techniques you already use.

Right-Brain Reports. Give learners the opportunity to work in small groups to create informational reports to present to the large group. Instead of verbally stating information, each small group uses one of the following right-brain reporting methods: song, rap, poem, dance,

movement, drama, art, sculpture, pantomime, skit, metaphor, improvisation, and so forth. When given the opportunity, participants can be phenomenally creative. Build in time for them to let their creativity shine. Use the activity Metaphor Magic to get started.

Stand, Walk, Talk. Balance learners' time of passive sitting and listening with active standing, walking, and talking. Learners can form standing groups while they review the material. They can move around the room while discussing the information they just learned. Include activities like the Walkabout and the Gallery Walk to add more movement to the training.

Brainstorming Time. Whenever possible, encourage learners to work collaboratively—in pairs, triads, small and large groups—to create a multitude of ways to solve problems, provide solutions, answer questions, collect facts, and think of new uses for learned material. Brainstorming, by definition, means that all answers are accepted for the time being so that the creative process isn't stifled by prematurely judging an idea as unworkable.

More Than One Right Answer. Expect learners to think of more than one right answer to any question you, or other learners, ask. The sixty-second Shout Outs are perfect for this purpose. With a Shout Out, learners have to come up with a number of correct answers, thus forcing them to continue thinking in more complex, creative ways.

Learner-Created Challenges. Have learners create their own questions, quizzes, and games. For example, working in table groups, each group can create a game such as Place Your Order or Grab That Spoon by using the material from the training. They exchange the games with the other groups so that they are playing a game that is different from the one their group created. Learners can also challenge each other with their own game-show questions and handmade quizzes.

Make It Outrageous. Ask yourself, What is the most outrageous thing I could do to get this point across and bring this point home? Or, What is the most outrageous thing I could have my training participants do so that they remember this information forever? Then do that thing, or a milder version of it, the next time you train.

Hang Out with Creative People. If you don't think you're creative enough, or if you find it hard to come up with a variety of creative training ideas, find yourself a couple of creative friends who do what you do, and learn from them. You can also take workshops, talk to other trainers, collect ideas, call friends with questions, and watch and learn. Give credit to those who teach you and pass the creativity on.

Trust Your Learners. It's truly amazing how creative a group of learners can be, if given half a chance. With a few guidelines to follow and a number of options to choose from, they will surprise you every time. So give them space, time, and opportunity to play with the training concepts, and see what they come up with.

The Linked Element

To make sure that learners link the new information with what they already know, choose from the following to include in your training.

Take a Minute. Linking new learning to old doesn't have to take up much training time, especially if you embed the linking throughout the training. Choose sixty-second activities that specifically ask learners to link what they are learning to what they already know.

Lecture the Links. During your lectures, be sure to point out how the new information fits with what learners already know (or what you think they may know) about the topic.

Use Games. Choose a game format, substitute your own content combined with what learners already know, and give them time to review new and old information by playing the game. Use five- and ten-minute games if you want short game formats.

Learner-Created Games. As with the creative element of CLUE, hand the game-making over to your training participants. Have them work in small groups to create board or card games by using all the topic-related information at hand. Then have groups exchange games and play. Show learners some of the "Take Five!" games like Place Your Order or Grab That Spoon as models of games they can make.

Talk About It. Always allow time for learners to discuss what they're learning and how it fits with what they know. The more dialogue time learners have, the deeper their linking will go, the greater their understanding, and the longer they will remember the information they learn.

The Useful Element

The more practical and useful you can make the training content, the more receptive participants will be to learning and using it afterwards. Add these suggestions to what you already have learners do.

Real-Life Challenges. Give learners real-life problems to solve. Small groups can each work on different challenges and then report their solutions to the whole group. Or small groups can discuss real-life problems they have encountered, write them down, and exchange them with other groups. Then each group brainstorms solutions and reports its findings to the whole class.

Demonstrations. Role plays are out—most training participants hate the thought of role plays. The word *demonstration* doesn't hold the same negative connotation for most learners. So give learners time to demonstrate how they could use the information. Small groups work to create demonstrations that could take the forms of skits, chart drawings, lists, presentations, news reports, 3-D sculptures, interviews, simulations, or whatever the learners think of that can show how they can use what they learned.

Improvisation. This is an activity that involves learners in a simulated, real-life situation without using rehearsed scripts. The purpose of the improvisation is to model or use the new training concepts. In it, you describe a real-life scene and ask for volunteers to take different parts of the action. You can stop the improvisation at any time to discuss what is happening, change characters, or step into it yourself. You can replay the scene by using different volunteers and different skills learned from the training. An improvisation is infinitely flexible in terms of whatever you want your learners to demonstrate. Two excellent sources for more improvisation suggestions are *Playing Along* (1997) by Izzy Gesell and *Improvisation, Inc.* (2000) by Robert Lowe.

Graffiti Wall. This is a large wall space covered with chart paper where training participants write ideas, questions, reactions, or comments on the paper with felt pens. Learners can also brainstorm and write ways to use the information they are learning. This is one of the many variations of the Gallery Walk.

Job-Shadowing. If possible, allow time for learners to observe how the training concepts and skills are being applied by shadowing someone who is actually using those concepts and skills. For example, if the training is about food service and the training site houses a cafeteria, participants could watch how other employees prepare food. If the training is about office skills, learners could watch how the office staff works.

Guest Speakers. Invite a person to speak who is already using the skills you are teaching. Allow time for learners to ask questions and to engage in a dialogue with this person.

Action Plans. Give learners time toward the end of the training to think, talk, and write about what they plan to do with what they learned. Use the Tickets Out or Action Plans to do this. When learners make a verbal or written commitment to use what they've learned after the training is over, there is a better chance that they will do just that: use it in some way. An action plan doesn't guarantee that training participants will follow up with applying the concepts to real-life situations, but it increases the probability that they will.

The Emotional Element

You already know that real learning only takes place when learners make positive emotional connections with the content and each other. Add these suggestions to what you already do to create positive learning experiences.

Connections Are the Keys. Creating psychological safety during a training is crucial for a positive emotional climate. Read again the section "Three Brains in One" to remind yourself of the importance of building a safe learning community. Always begin your training with connections: connecting learners to what they already know, to what they want to learn, to each other, and to you.

Keep Them Going. Connections don't just happen at the beginning of your training. Your learners need to keep the positive connections going throughout the entire learning experience. They do this through the training activities and games you include. They also do this through collaborative learning strategies: small group discussions, paired and triad learning, and group projects and presentations.

Right to Pass. When you give learners the right to observe an activity instead of having to participate in it, you also give them permission to take care of their own emotional well-being. This has the effect of increasing the feeling of safety, since they have the choice of participating or not. Often this simple step is enough to dissipate any resistance to the learning.

Need-to-Know Guidelines. Sometimes specific behavioral guidelines are necessary for psychological safety. These guidelines are the need-to-knows about what is acceptable behavior and speech during the training—and what isn't. One example is the guideline "No putdowns." Since teasing can often move quickly from friendly to hurtful, another guideline might be: "When in doubt, leave it out." A caveat: Don't ever assume that just because people work or go to school together, they feel psychologically safe with each other. Stating or posting a few simple behavioral guidelines at the beginning of a training can help maintain psychological safety.

What's Your Baggage? Every person walking into a training room brings along his own emotional baggage, that is, the thoughts and behaviors that cause the downshifting into emotional and survival brains. Trainers are no exception. Be aware of the emotional triggers you carry within—things that upset you or beliefs that, if challenged, make you defensive. Know that learners can pick up your emotional state of being just as you can pick up theirs. Once you know your own emotional baggage, you can deal with it on a conscious level—by changing the way you talk to yourself about it or by changing the circumstances that cause you to downshift. You can also be aware of what triggers your learners and change parts of your training to make them feel more at ease.

Sarcasm Is Out. No matter what anyone tells you, sarcasm is always disguised anger. As was stated earlier, "When in doubt, leave it out." If a learner's way of teasing others feels sarcastic to you, it probably is. You may need to talk with the person privately about the sarcasm.

Take Care of It Now. When you notice a problem in the training that is causing negative emotions among learners, stop to address it. This can be done privately, one-on-one, within the small group where the problem lies, or with the whole group as part of a solution-seeking process. Sometimes just checking in with the person or people involved (for example, saying, "This is what I see happening. What is going on?") is enough to change the situation. Once in awhile, ignoring a negative situation works and the problem disappears. More often, ignoring something only makes it worse. Watch for the effects that a negative situation has on the learners, and decide on the options you have in choosing how to handle the situation. A word to the wise: Never sacrifice the group for the sake of an individual. It is always hurtful for the group.

Go with Your Gut. Pause at different times during the training and become aware of both overt and covert emotional nuances in the group (body language, voice tone, words, actions, and so on). By doing this, you will understand the emotional state of most of your learners. If your intuition tells you something is amiss, pay attention to it. It simply means the intuitive right brain is picking up signals that the logical left brain is missing.

Be Careful of Pain. Some trainers say they begin with an uncomfortable experience in order for learners to perceive a need, that is, the need to stop the discomfort by learning what it is the trainer wants them to learn. Or sometimes trainers include role plays that are uncomfortable for the same reason. A word of caution is in order: If you do this, remember the *triune brain* and move quickly from pain to pleasure. Too much downshifting means you will lose your learners entirely as they move from thinking brain into emotional and survival brains.

Tips and Variations!

Create a Trainer's Toolbag. Gather a collection of interesting training strategies and write out and put them in one place—a binder, file folder, or a metaphoric bag, toolbox, toolkit, "trainer's treasures"—someplace where you can access them easily and quickly. Whenever you come across a teaching or learning method that you like, add it to your collection. Sharpen your observation skills as you notice new ideas, activities, and materials that other trainers use.

Vary Your Training Tools. Some of the strategies you use are your standard, signature methods—activities you include all the time. Others are ones you use for awhile and then put away because they have become boring both to you and the participants. Keep a variety of strategies at hand and rotate them so that they remain as fresh for you as for the learners. Always ask yourself, "Why am I choosing this training method to use? Is there a better way for learners to get this material?" Often you'll find that the only reason you're sticking with old strategies is because they are the ones you're most comfortable with, not because they're the best ones.

It's About Them First. Throughout the training, give learners time to discuss what they already know about the training topic, and time to talk about how the new learning fits with the old. Use a variety of "Got a Minute?" and "Take Five!" activities to do this.

The Important Question. The bottom line to any training is simply, *how can the learners use this in the real world?* Keep asking that question for every concept you teach. If you don't know the answer, find out. Once you have the answer, tie everything you teach to it. You can also encourage learners to answer the question for themselves.

Keep It Positive. Training participants always want more of a positive learning experience and less of a negative one. Positive doesn't mean everyone agrees with each other. Positive means that everyone is part of a learning community in which each person is respected. There can still be disagreement, challenge, and intensity in the learning. It just doesn't need to lead to psychological danger (see the section "Three Brains in One" in Part Two for more on the need for safety in learning).

Wrapping It Up

When you make your training creative, linked, useful, and emotional, you not only motivate training participants to become involved in their own learning but you also help move that learning into long-term memory. Probably the best benefit from the four CLUE elements is that learners will associate learning with positive feelings and want more of what makes them feel good. It's a win-win for everyone—for you, the learners, their company or school, and for the larger world they inhabit.

When your soul is happy, your learning is snappy!
—Dave Meier

Early to Finish

Action Plan. Think about the four CLUE elements. In the space below, list a few activities you already use that incorporate some or all of these elements. Then go back through this chapter and circle one more suggestion for each element—ideas you plan to use in your next training.

You Said It But Did They Get It?

How to Check for Understanding

Picture This

You just finished facilitating a customer service training for a small group of your company's employees. They listened attentively the whole time you were talking. A few of them even took some notes.

Now you stop and ask, "Do you understand?" They nod their heads. You continue, "Do you have any questions?" They shake their heads. "Good," you think, "they've got it."

Or do they? During the next few days, these employees make a number of service mistakes that cause you to wonder, "Didn't they hear what I told them? If they had only listened, they'd know the right thing to do." You end up spending precious time helping them correct their mistakes and reviewing the information you already gave them. Meanwhile, your company loses productive time (and perhaps a customer or two) while you reteach and retrain.

What Is Checking for Understanding?

Checking for understanding simply means *you stop talking and ask learners to say or do something* with the information you just gave them. According to author Madeline Hunter (*Enhancing Teaching*, 2003), you should check for understanding after you've presented an important piece of information. By doing this, you'll know immediately whether learners understand what they just heard. You'll also know whether you need to reteach any of the concepts you've presented. And you can correct any comprehension errors the instant they arise, instead of waiting for a review time later in the training.

What Does Checking for Understanding Do?

When you check for understanding, you

- *Have* learners say or do something with what they've learned.
- *Listen* to their words and observe their behaviors—both good indicators of whether they understand the material they just learned.
- *Gain* an understanding of how well learners will be able to apply what they've learned in their own jobs and lives.
- *Decide* whether you need to reteach or review specific training material.
- *Can feel* confident that learners will remember the information after the training is over.

Five Activities to Check for Understanding

Repeat Back. Ask learners to repeat aloud to you or to another learner what they just heard you say. Or tell them to paraphrase what they learned, using their own words to explain it. Or they can form small groups and tell their group members the three most important things they remember from the material. Listen to their conversations and encourage them to give each other corrective feedback.

Think Back. Ask learners to think about the new information and how it fits with what they already know. Invite them to share a comment or a question about what they heard you say. Tell them to take turns stating one way they might be able to use the new information in work situations. According to David Meier (*The Accelerated Learning Handbook,* 2000), learners need time "to reflect on experience and to create connections, meanings, and values" out of new information.

Teach Back. Author Richard Bach in *Illusions* (1977) reminds us, "We master what we teach." Give learners time to teach each other in order to master the material. They can do this in pairs, with one person acting as the teacher and the other acting as the student. The teacher explains the concepts to the student. Then they switch roles. They also give each other corrective feedback. Refer to the Each One Teach One activity for more ideas.

Play Back. Do a short improvisation with the participants, using both yourself and volunteers to demonstrate important concepts you've just taught. Read the *useful* element ideas in the "Get a CLUE!" chapter for more improvisation ideas. The Play Back can last just a few minutes. It can be humorous or dramatic. More important, it can reveal how well training participants are able to apply the new information to a specific work situation.

Report Back. After a training session ends, learners need to apply the new information to specific work situations, evaluate the results, report the results to the trainer or another qualified colleague, and get feedback from that person. Author Sivasailam "Thiagi" Thiagarajan (*Design Your Own Games and Activities,* 2003), says, "Learners cannot master skills without repeated practice and relevant feedback." Arrange to have learners check back with you after the training, either in person or through e-mail or phone calls. Find out how they used the information they learned, what the results were, and whether they encountered any difficulties along the way. Ask them to evaluate themselves, and then add your comments to theirs. Give them positive feedback, as well as suggestions for using the concepts or skills in more effective ways. Also have them do peer coaching, that is, they give corrective feedback to each other.

¡Tips and Variations!

Watch and Listen. Listen to the learners' conversations and observe their behaviors as they participate in an activity that checks for understanding.

Reteach Right Away. Include these activities throughout your training so that you can immediately review and reteach any concepts that are unclear to the learners.

Discuss It. Follow the activities with a few minutes of whole group processing in which participants talk about what they learned from the activity and what other questions or concerns they may still have.

Wrapping It Up

When you check for understanding, you make sure that learners not only hear the concepts but also understand them and are able to apply them to specific work situations. When learners say and do something with what they've learned, they will feel confident that they have the skills to use the new information when they need to—which is what real learning is all about.

What is expressed by the learner is often more important than what is expressed to the learner.

—Win Wenger

Early to Finish

Action Plan. Review the five activities in this section. Choose two that you plan to use in your next training. Draw a box around each and label them #1 and #2, in order of importance to you.

What's a Picture Worth?

The Importance of Imagery in Learning

Quick Start

Just Think: As you slowly read each phrase below, pay attention to what is going on in your mind:

Pink elephants	Running a race	9/11
Ocean waves	Christmas tree	Your first love
Reading a book	Jungle tigers	Favorite family member

It's safe to say that you instantly translated the words into mental pictures. You didn't think of the words themselves—that is, the printed sequence of letters—but rather you thought of what the words represent: an animal, an action, an emotional experience, a particular person or thing. Your mind knew, without your having to tell it so, that a word is simply a representation of an image. And an image is a representation of either something observed in physical reality or a mental concept or idea.

In this chapter, you will explore why images are important in learning and how to include them in your training.

Picture This

You are attending a train-the-trainer workshop. The training room you enter looks nothing like most corporate training rooms. Hanging at odd angles on the walls are colorful charts with training reminders printed in large, bold lettering and illustrated with cartoons.

On the round tables for participants are cheery centerpieces of multicolored paper, fanned out so that participants can use them as note-taking sheets. The trainer, Sharon, welcomes you and gives you a packet of printed materials. You notice that each page contains a graphic or cartoon representing the main idea of that section. You also notice that there are a number of note-taking pages in the materials—pages with blank geometric shapes, columns, and empty spaces for you to fill in later. Sharon calls them "graphic organizers."

As the workshop progresses, Sharon invites you to take notes in a pictorial format by using doodles and symbols as well as words. Every slide or transparency she displays has a colorful illustration of the concept she is presenting. She also illustrates her lectures with short stories and real-life examples so that you get a mental picture of what she is explaining. Many times she links information to body movements, inviting everyone to participate in the movement while repeating the information. Although the participants laugh while they participate, you realize later that it's easier for you to remember certain facts because of the physical movement associated with them.

Toward the end of the training, Sharon tells the table groups to choose a right-brain way of summarizing what they learned. She posts a list of presentation methods to choose from: illustration, metaphor, skit, story, demonstration, dance, poem, rap, song, clay sculpture, and the like. She gives you time to review the information and work with your group on your summary.

After each group presents its unusual summary and receives a round of applause, Sharon talks about various ways of using imagery to help learners remember important information. You realize you just experienced at least a half-dozen of these image-making techniques. This train-the-trainer workshop has been an image-rich learning experience that you will remember for a long time to come.

The Two-Sided Brain

When we use the terms *right brain* or *left brain,* we are referring to the two sides of the cerebrum, neocortex, or thinking brain. The research about these two brain hemispheres began in the early 1960s with studies of epileptic patients. From intensive experimentation, doctors discovered that each side of the neocortex is somewhat specialized, with  the left hemisphere processing most verbal language and the right hemisphere processing most visual images. The left side also thinks in a more sequential, step-by-step, logical, concrete, black-and-white way, whereas the right side thinks in a more holistic, intuitive, random, emotive, three-dimensional, Technicolor way.

Although these are generalities, they are useful in helping us understand why images are important to learning.

Obviously, for learning to stick, we need to engage both sides of the thinking brain "to get the complete picture," so to speak. And usually, both sides work simultaneously to help us do just that: *both sides work together to help us understand and remember information on multiple levels and in multiple ways.*

Even if we are familiar with this brain hemisphere research, we also know that most formal learning places (for example, college classrooms and corporate training rooms) still emphasize word-saturated, left-brain teaching techniques and include very few image-rich, right-brain learning methods. We need to go back in time to understand why this is so.

The Roles of Images and Words

Before the advent of the printing press in the 1400s, most humans learned through concrete experience (the physical body with its sensory-rich learning) and oral language using right-brain teaching and learning methods: ballads, poetry, songs, stories, anecdotes, plays, and the like. They also used visual ways to learn: drawing, painting, imagining, and creating icons, shapes, and sculptures to represent ideas. Books were few and far between and definitely unavailable to the masses.

By the 1500s, when books became mass-produced and widespread throughout Europe, learning moved from an image-rich, concrete experience to a word-rich representation of a concrete experience. David Meier in *The Accelerated Learning Handbook* (2000) says it best: "As the book became the major vehicle for education, learning came to emphasize a mechanical, linear, one-thing-at-a-time process . . . the printing press elevated words over images . . . and the left brain over the right" (pp. 27, 157).

By the 1800s, most Western cultures had shifted to predominantly book-based systems of formal schooling. It stayed that way for the most part until the end of the twentieth century. But profound changes began taking place from the late 1950s until the present, largely because of the one learning tool—television—that, for better or worse, has held the most influence over how we take in information today.

Television has moved whole cultures from the power of words back to the power of images to teach, to persuade, to excite, to make memorable. Advertisers know this. More and more commercials are a series of split-second images strung together in rapid-fire sequence, sometimes with verbal or written language accompanying them, and sometimes not. Another example is *Sesame Street*—children's educational television that makes use of these short snippets of visual and verbal information delivered quickly, one right after the other. Movie producers also do this: they use "trailers"—a dozen short scenes flashed in quick succession from the movie itself—to entice viewers to watch that particular movie.

Whether or not we feel this return to the image as a teaching tool is a bad or good thing is not the issue. The important point to keep in mind is that the brain thinks in both words and images. As David Meier writes: "True learning is a matter of both/and—both books and experience, both words and images, both left brain and right, both sequential and simultaneous processing, both abstract reflection and concrete experience" (2000, p. 27).

Sometimes we, as trainers, just need to be reminded that we already know this. When we make our training image-rich, we increase the probability that learners will remember the information longer than if we use words alone to teach.

Take a Break

Doodles: Using symbols, lines, or cartoons, quickly represent each of the following concepts with an image. A reminder: this isn't about art but about remembering concepts longer.

Concept	Image
Attention Maker, Breaker	
Three Brains in One	
The Learning Compass	
The Training Map	

What Is Imagery?

Imagery is any teaching method that helps the brain form mental pictures to represent what is being learned. Generally speaking, when you lecture without using any image-making method, learners are limited to processing the spoken information in the main language center of the thinking brain—the left hemisphere only. Put another way, you are teaching to half the brain, while the other half sits pretty much idle.

But when you include training methods that are image-rich, you not only make the information more interesting to the learner, you also make it more memorable. Image-rich tools include:

- Storytelling and anecdotes
- Metaphors and analogies
- Doodles, cartoons, and photos
- Symbols, shapes, and icons
- Movement and gestures
- Physical objects
- Videos and any other visual aids

In addition to the above, you can also encourage training participants to draw their own visual symbols for the information—doodles, shapes, lines, simple drawings, icons, symbols—to help them remember important concepts. You can remind them that it's not about drawing skills. It's about memory skills. And you can empower them to create their own personal memory tools.

What Does Imagery Do?

By including imagery in your training, you will

- *Make* your lectures more interesting.
- *Ensure* that the information will be easier for your learners to remember later.
- *Deepen* the learners' understanding of important concepts.
- *Save* yourself, and your learners, training time that would have been spent in lengthy lectures.
- *Encourage* learners to make their own visual memory aids.

- *Move* learning into learners' long-term memory.
- *Become* comfortable with right-brain ways of delivering information (for you) and right-brain ways of retaining information (for your learners).

Ways to Use Imagery in Training

Tell Stories. The easiest way to begin using images is to tell a short story to illustrate a concept. Make up a story or use one that you've heard (please cite the source when you do this). Only include stories that relate to the training content. Add a little drama to the storytelling with voice tone, pauses, gestures, and movement. Practice telling the story in private so that you are comfortable reciting it in front of a group. For more information on how to tell a story, use the fabulous book by Mary Wacker and Lori Silverman (2003), *Stories Trainers Tell*. This book offers insights into creating and telling your own stories, as well as a collection of fifty-five ready-made trainers' stories you can use. If you're uncomfortable or just a bit rusty with storytelling, this resource will quickly sharpen your skills.

Use Physical Space. Designate a portion of the physical space near you to represent a fact or a procedural step. Then point to that space whenever you reference that concept. For example, if you're teaching a three-step safety procedure, point to the left side of the room for the first step, the middle for the second, and the right for the third step. Then ask the learners to state which step is represented by which space in the room. As you continue the lecture, gesture to each of the spaces to reinforce the steps. This gives learners a spatial way to remember information, that is, a visual reminder that uses three-dimensional space.

Use Movement. Linking a fact or concept to a physical gesture, motion, or body part is a powerful way to move learning into long-term memory. An example of this is in the introduction to Part Three of this book, where you learned the Four Levels of Training Competence by linking them to four body parts or areas—hips, shoulders, head, overhead—and you moved your hands from one part to another. A second example is in the "Three Brains in One" chapter of Part Two, where you used your wrist, fist, hand, and motions to represent brain parts and downshifting. A third example is in the "Let the Compass Be Your Guide" chapter in Part Two: you used arm motions to remember the four compass points and what they stood for.

   Make up your own motions for important facts or procedural steps. Memorize them until you are comfortable enough to teach them easily and quickly. Have your participants do them with you, and repeat them up to six times during the training to reinforce the concepts.

Use Graphics. Whenever possible, illustrate your charts, slides, overheads, or hand-out material with clip art or cartoons. Do a Web search on www.google.com for free, downloadable computer clip art. Or join www.clipart.com, a pay-for-use clip art Web site that contains thousands of cartoons, graphics, and symbols that you are allowed to use when you pay the basic fee. Be aware of copyright issues with syndi-cated cartoons in newspapers and magazines—check with your own company poli-cy regarding such issues, or do a copyright search on the Internet for international copyright laws.

Draw Doodles. In addition to using computer graphics, create a few simple doo-dles of your own to represent certain concepts. Practice drawing them on chart paper or on an overhead transparency until you can do so quickly, easily, and while talking at the same time. Then, when you introduce each concept, draw the doodle that goes with it. Learners can draw it with you or copy it after you've drawn it. A great resource to help you get started is *A Picture's Worth 1,000 Words: A Workbook for Visual Communications,* by Jean Westcott and Jennifer Landau (1997). The book is packed with quick, easy, can-do and ready-to-use ideas for visually enhancing any training.

Encourage Learners to Doodle. As you lecture, invite learners to create their own doodles to represent certain concepts. Provide colored paper, index cards, or Post-it® notes as doodling material. Use colored pens, felt pens, or pencils. Have learners explain their doodles to each other so that they reinforce the concepts rep-resented by the doodles. Use the Doodle activities in Part One to do this.

Use Metaphors. Anytime you use a metaphor or an analogy—an illustration comparing the concept you're teaching with an object or idea unrelated to the concept—you are using a powerful image-making technique. Metaphors can be stories, pictures, or actual objects you bring to the training. You can also invite learners to create and explain their own metaphors for the training concepts. Refer to the Metaphor Magic activity in Part One for more ways to use metaphors.

Use Graphic Organizers. These are handout pages that you have created before-hand and that learners use when they are listening and taking notes. In other words, they are structured ways for training participants to take notes by using shapes, bubbles, lines, and columns, as well as doodles and words. One example is a page with simple vertical columns that are labeled: facts, questions, doodles. Another example is a mind map, that is, a cluster of blank shapes around a central concept. Learners fill in the shapes with facts about the concept as you lecture. Learners can also create their own graphic organizers. The best source for ideas is the book *Graphic Organizers,* by Karen Bromley, Linda Irwin-De Vitis, and Marcia Modlo (1995). There are also a number of sample graphic organizers at the end of this section of *The Ten-Minute Trainer* to help get you started using this kind of note-taking.

¡ Tips and Variations !

Baby Steps First. If you're uncomfortable including images while training, then choose only one or two imagery tools to use at a time. For example, you may have a cartoon that is topic related. In addition to that, you might have a topic-related story to share. When you're comfortable with those two tools, add another image to your training—perhaps a metaphor, a photo, or a certain gesture that represents a key point. Keep experimenting with different ways of creating mental pictures to help training participants grasp the concepts in right-brain ways.

It's Not About Art. Remind yourself that it doesn't matter what the doodles look like—what matters is helping your learners remember key concepts. Whatever you draw, and whatever your learners draw, is about engaging the right brain in the learning.

The Gallery Walk. Use this Part One activity to include learner-created visual images. Instead of writing words on the wall charts, direct learners to draw images, icons, symbols, or doodles first and then label their drawings afterwards.

The Graffiti Wall Revisited. For this variation on the Gallery Walk, simply cover one wall with a number of blank chart pages and invite participants to represent training concepts with drawings. They can label their drawings if they wish. Again, drawings can be stick figures, doodles, icons, symbols, geometric shapes, or flow charts—anything other than words.

Images with Accelerated Learning. David Meier's *The Accelerated Learning Handbook* (2000) has two awesome chapters on using imagery in training: "Pictograms" (p. 133) and "Imagery and Learning" (p. 157). Both chapters offer dozens of ideas to incorporate imagery in a variety of unusual ways.

Wrapping It Up

The human brain and television both have one great commonality: imagery. One relies on images to learn. The other relies on images to educate, entertain, and persuade. As trainers, we need to use image-rich language and training methods to make our training more interesting and more memorable. When participants use both sides of their thinking brain to learn, the probability increases of remembering and using the information later. In other words, we can teach it more quickly, and make it stick longer, with imagery.

Following this chapter are a number of sample graphic organizers. Feel free to use them any way you wish. You can also add to them or change them to better fit the concepts you are teaching.

Ah, if you could dance all that you've just said,
then I'd understand.
—Nikos Kazanztakis in *Zorba the Greek*

The soul never thinks without a picture.
—Plato

Early to Finish

More Doodles. Skim Parts One and Two again to find the ideas that really appealed to you. Draw doodles in the page margins to represent those important ideas. Your drawings can also be stars, checkmarks, arrows, or attention-getting shapes to remind you that these facts are important to you.

Sample Graphic Organizers

Instructions: Use the following simple, note-taking pages as graphic organizer templates (please cite the source) or as ideas you can use to spark more creative graphic organizers of your own.

List It Here!

Topic: _____

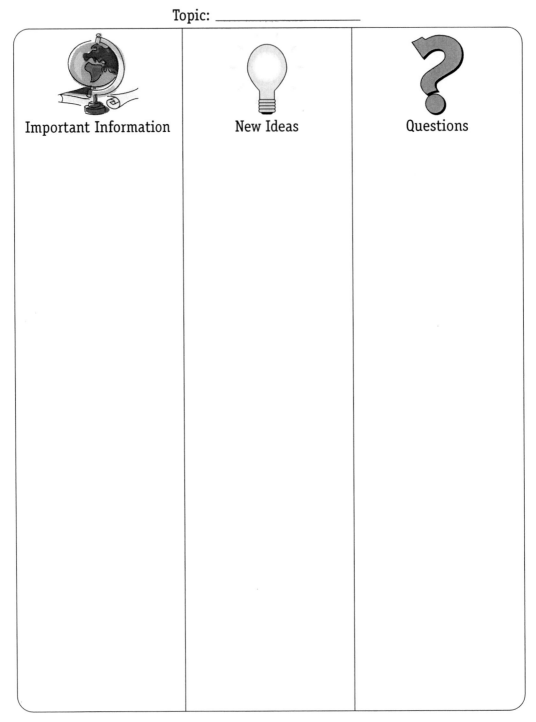

Important Information	New Ideas	Questions

It's in the Bag!

Topic: _____

Mapping the Miles

Topic: _____

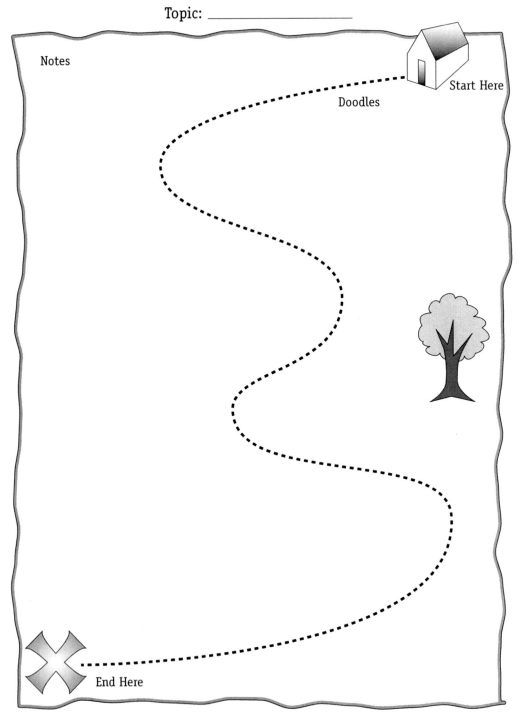

Notes

Start Here

Doodles

End Here

The Ten-Minute Trainer

Nifty Notes

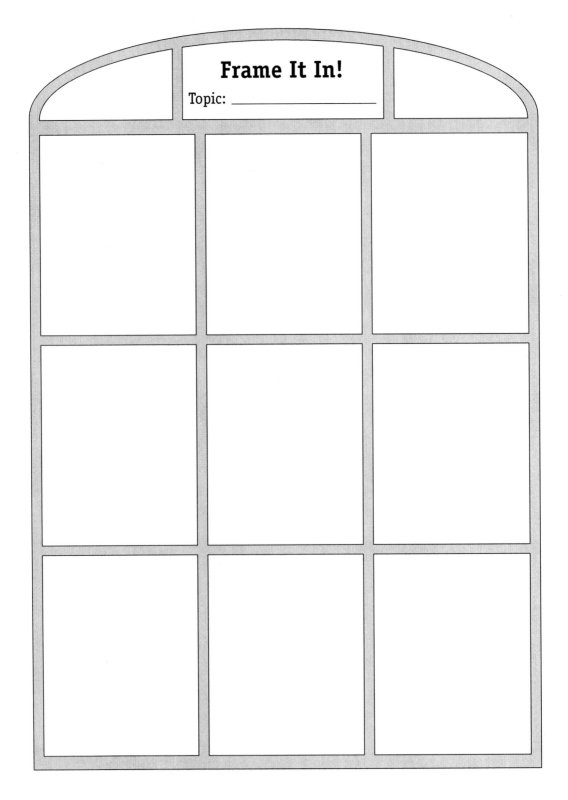

Frame It In!

Topic: _____

Word Wall

Topic: _____

Modified and reprinted with permission from Cliff St. Germain, Ph.D., *Study Whiz,* 2000.

Clips

Topic: _____

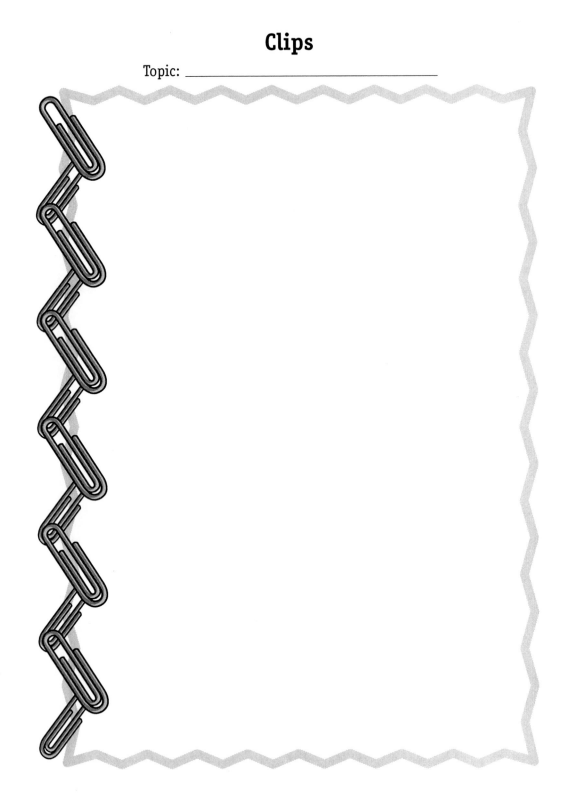

Scribbles:

Notes Along the Way:

The Ten-Minute Trainer

Station Rotation
Learning a Lot in a Little Time

Quick Start

Pop-Ups: Try a little experiment. Focus your mind on your energy level right now. Then pop up (that is, stand up), walk across the room, and sit in another chair. It might sound silly, but do this two more times. Then pay attention to your physical energy level. You probably feel more energized because you've been standing up and moving around the room instead of remaining seated in one place for that length of time.

Learners feel the same way when they do a Station Rotation. Their bodies are physically energized from the activities and movement while their minds remain alert and interested in the tasks at each station. In this chapter, we'll explore this unique training activity.

Picture This

It is the second day of a two-day workshop on communication skills. The day before, the six rectangular tables for participants were set up in two columns with an aisle down the middle of the room. Now the tables jut out perpendicularly from the side walls, three tables to a side. The tables are marked in order with signs that say, "Station One, Station Two, Station Three . . ." up to "Station Six." Posted on the wall above each table is a chart paper with the station activity instructions printed on it. One table holds game materials, another writing materials. One table is full of craft items.

When the thirty participants arrive, instructor Julio assigns each person a number from one to six. Participants find the table with their number and sit at it. Julio explains the Station Rotation purpose and process. At each of four stations, participants will be practicing a communication skill they learned about the day before. At the fifth and sixth stations, they will be doing a creative project and learning a new communication skill. They will spend ten minutes at each station and will have thirty seconds to rotate clockwise between each station table. Julio will use upbeat music to signal each rotation time.

The Station Rotation activities begin. The groups read their instructions and participate in their station activity. At the first station, group members pair up and practice active listening skills. At the second station, they play a communication board game, asking and answering questions about effective communication. At the third station, they practice giving each other corrective feedback. At the fourth station, they work individually to write a communication problem on an index card, then read, discuss, and solve the problems as a group. At the fifth station, they use the craft materials to create three-dimensional metaphors for a communication concept they consider important. At the sixth station, Julio teaches them a short lesson on a new communication skill called "Checking for Understanding."

When the Station Rotation time ends, the whole group takes a short break. After the break, station groups take turns displaying and explaining their three-dimensional communication metaphors. Everyone applauds each station group.

Finally, to process the Station Rotation activities, Julio leads a whole group discussion by asking a series of questions: "Which activity challenged you the most? Which activity did you learn the most from? What did you learn about yourself? What knowledge and skills will you use back at work because of these activities? What is one question you still have concerning any of the Station Rotation content?" Julio ends the discussion by thanking everyone for participating. He hands out Station Rotation certificates of completion and joins the whole group in one last round of applause.

What Is a Station Rotation?

A Station Rotation is really a series of short activities that learners can do in a certain sequence during one portion of the training day, or interspersed throughout the day. The short activities all take place at the same time in different parts of the training room. In small groups, learners rotate from activity to activity, following the written or audiotaped instructions at each activity  table or station. All activities are built around concepts taught during the training. All activities introduce, review, or apply these concepts in various ways.

The Ten-Minute Trainer

What Does a Station Rotation Do?

By participating in Station Rotation activities, learners can

- *Review* previously learned information in a variety of short, quick ways.
- *Teach* themselves some new, topic-related information.
- *Practice* topic-related skills for a short time.
- *Coach* and give feedback to each other as they practice skills.
- *Do* self-assessment inventories.
- *Quiz* each other about what they've learned.
- *Link* new learning to old, and draw on what they already know.
- *Play* a topic-related game.
- *Plan* a project or do some self-study.
- *Create* a short presentation using the concepts they've learned.
- *Keep* both their minds and bodies awake and alert as they physically move around the room.
- *Increase* motivation and interest as well as learning and retention as they experience this unique way of learning.
- *Apply* what they have learned in challenging, interesting, and creative ways.

 Getting Ready

Materials: The materials you need will depend upon what activities you decide to have at each station. For example, if participants play a game at one station, be sure to have all necessary game materials there. Also, make sure there are enough materials for all rotation groups. At a writing station, for example, have enough writing materials for everyone. Or at a craft station, have sufficient craft items for all groups. With art materials, one option is to fill a number of small lunch bags with specific items, and instruct each group to use one bagful of materials. Craft materials can include: construction paper, scissors, crayons, modeling clay, Play-Doh®, dowel sticks, feathers, string, glue, stickers, Legos™, pipe cleaners, tongue depressors, Styrofoam shapes, and the like.

Setup: Decide how many stations you want and designate certain tables or break-out areas for the stations. Choose an activity for each station. Activities can include: games, puzzles, worksheets, discussion questions, reading assignments, skills practice in pairs or as a group, individual or group self-corrected tests, charts or diagrams to make, flashcards to review, direct instruction from you or an assistant, or presentations or skits to prepare. Figure out the approximate time it will take for participants to complete most of the activities. Post each station activity set of instructions on a chart paper, a handout, or a taped recording located at or near the station.

Group Size: Station groups can be as small as two or as large as eight people per group. An optimum number is to have one station for every four to six participants, but you can certainly adjust the numbers to accommodate your goals.

Time: Station Rotation activities work best when they are from five to twenty minutes in length. The time allotted will depend upon the type of activities you choose to include. The time length will need to be the same for all stations if all groups rotate at the same time. Allow about thirty seconds' rotation time between stations. Choose a rotation signal to use. It may be high-energy music, a noise-maker, flashing the room lights, or simply saying "Time to rotate." Upbeat music is the most fun signal, as it lightens the mood and energizes the learners as they move around the room. Time for the entire Station Rotation process will vary depending upon the time allotted for the stations and for a whole group discussion about the activity outcomes afterwards.

Special Note: This activity is somewhat complex and takes careful preparation. Double-check materials, instructions, and procedures. Allow yourself and your learners to make some mistakes as you get comfortable with the activity. If necessary, feel free to stop the Station Rotation and adjust the timing or station activities. If you are new to training, you might want to wait until you have more experience before using this activity.

Station Rotation Instructions

• Explain the purpose of the Station Rotation process (introducing new material, reviewing learned material, applying what has been learned, and so forth). Give participants a short overview of each station activity and a description of what they will be doing.

- Tell participants how groups will rotate (clockwise, counterclockwise, randomly), the time allotted for each station, and what the rotation signal is. Let participants know what they need to take with them and what to do if they finish early (one option is to post a list of Early to Finish suggestions such as questions to discuss, note-taking ideas, or topic-related material to read).
- Divide the whole group into station groups. One way to do this is to have participants count off by the number of stations and then go to the station with the same number. Let them know that they will be staying with their small group as they rotate from station to station.
- Begin the Station Rotation process and time each rotation (or assign someone to do this). While the activities are going on, walk around the room and monitor the station groups, answer questions, and offer assistance if necessary. Pay attention to the station time allotted. If it seems too short or too long for most of the groups, then change it to fit the needs of the majority.
- When participants have rotated through all the stations, announce a short break and then discuss the station activities with the whole group. Be sure to allow enough time for processing the entire learning experience. Discussion questions can include:

Which activity challenged you the most?

From which activity did you learn the most? Which was the most meaningful for you?

What were three important things you learned from the activities?

What did you learn about yourself? About others?

What are three take-aways for you from the entire Station Rotation process?

What knowledge and skills will you use back at work because of these activities?

What is your action plan as a result of these activities?

What is one question you still have concerning any of the Station Rotation material?

- Have participants acknowledge and celebrate their station groups with kudos, applause, handshakes, or high-fives.

¡Tips and Variations!

Station Breaks. Instead of doing all the Station Rotation activities sequentially during a specific chunk of time, scatter them throughout your training day by having small groups go to different stations as breaks between lecture segments. For example, after a lecture segment of about ten to twenty minutes, each table group goes to a different station and does the activity there for about five minutes. Afterwards, groups return to their original tables and you lecture again until the next Station Break. Before the training ends, process the Station Rotation activities with the whole group.

Activity Rotation. Instead of rotating groups through the stations, rotate the activities among table groups. Make sure that everything needed to do each station activity is in a large manila envelope or small box, and pass the envelopes or boxes from table to table.

Station Rotation Table. Display all the Station Rotation activities on one table (activities are in manila envelopes or boxes that include all instructions and materials). During a Station Break, each table group chooses an activity to do. They return all envelopes and boxes to the Station Rotation table when done. Later, they choose a different one. Or give them enough time during a Station Break to do two or three activities.

Learner-Created Stations. Each table group makes up a Station Rotation activity complete with all necessary materials and instructions. Then groups rotate through all tables except their own. For example, for a restaurant class, one table group creates a game like Place Your Order for the procedure to follow when serving guests. Another group creates a list of food preparation skills for groups to choose from and demonstrate. A third group creates a Myth or Fact game about kitchen appliances. A fourth group makes a Grab That Spoon game with question and answer cards about food preparation.

Early to Finish. Post a list of Early to Finish ideas from Part One so that groups that finish early can choose something to do while they wait.

Group-Created Processing. Have station groups lead the processing afterwards, making up the discussion questions and facilitating the whole group discussion. Guide the discussion with some of your own processing questions, too.

Create Your Own!

Use the box below to jot down your own Station Rotation ideas.

Closing and Celebration

So Now You Know!

Celebrating Your Journey with
The Ten-Minute Trainer

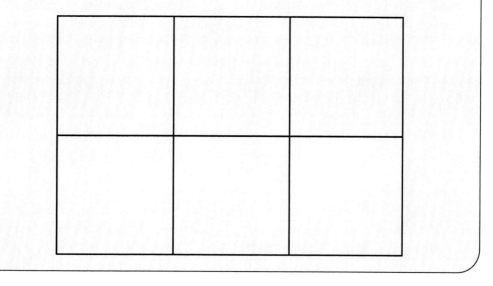

Quick Start

Blackout Bingo: In the squares below, write six ideas (one per square) from this book that you are planning to use in future training programs. If a family member is handy, explain the six ideas to him or her. Or call a training colleague and tell that person what the six ideas are. You can also write brief definitions on another paper. After you explain or define each item, put a star or checkmark in each square and write "Blackout Bingo!" across the page.

Training isn't about perfection. It's about process—the process of learning. And learning is messy stuff. The learning journey is a bumpy one, filled with obstacles, crooked trails, hills, valleys, and sometimes spectacular, mountaintop vistas where we see the grand view of a learning goal finally achieved.

An educator once said, "I would be such a great teacher if it weren't for the kids!" We can make the most logical lesson plans, using everything we know about good teaching and training, and still sometimes it all goes to Hades in a handbasket. *Nothing works all the time.* Sometimes we let go of everything we know and go with our gut, that is, trust our intuition to guide us home. During those times, we take a deep breath, say a silent prayer, and simply walk in faith that it will all turn out well for ourselves and for our learners.

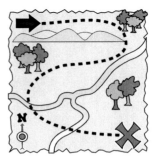

Claim What You Know

That said, you have now come full circle, back to the two fundamental principles on which *The Ten-Minute Trainer* is based: *shorter segments of instruction are better than longer ones, and learners remember more when they are involved in the learning.* You show both colleagues and learners that these concepts are what you value by practicing what you preach and by modeling these concepts every step of the way.

You realize now that there are many reasons for embracing these two concepts—reasons such as television-dominated cultures, shorter attention spans, image-rich learning, and brain research that supports the need for learners to talk, move, create, question, and to feel safe instead of threatened.

You know how to honor your learners—respecting them, their desires for learning, what they already know, and their need to personally connect with the training concepts, with each other, and with you. You know how to motivate, inspire, and involve your learners by offering a learning experience that is *creative*, *linked* to what they know, *useful* to them, and that feels *emotionally positive* and satisfying.

You also use time in different ways now, knowing how powerful precious minutes can be in moving learning into long-term memory. You honor your own time—designing and delivering training in more time-efficient ways so that you do, indeed, have a life after training.

And "you know that you know," that is, you can now take all you've learned from *The Ten-Minute Trainer* and make it your own, add your own artistry to it, and teach it to others.

The Jewel of the Journey

There is a treasure embedded in every training journey. There is a hidden jewel that you'll find regardless of whether you're even looking for it. This treasure makes the journey worthwhile, even during the most difficult training times. Just reminding yourself of this gem is an energy boost and helps you reaffirm why you're a learning facilitator in the first place.

Spend a moment now taking it in—this sparkling truth about who you are and what you do:

You are part of a profound change
in how humans teach each other
and learn from each other.
You are part of a profound shift
of human consciousness
about the acts of teaching and learning.
You are changing the old patterns
of giving and receiving knowledge
so that all teachers, trainers, and
learning facilitators will know how to
honor their learners, respect their learners,
and hand the learning back to their learners.
By doing this, learners will grow
in knowledge, in wisdom,
and in action that is meaningful to them.
Because you have had faith in them,
they will have faith in themselves.
Nothing less than this:
learners and teachers together,
changing and growing together,
moving toward wisdom together,
an amazing journey together!

Handing It Back to the Learner

As a trainer, you are moving in the direction of not teaching what you know, but drawing knowledge out of your learners so that they can, in fact, teach themselves. You stand as their guide, ready to help when asked, but also ready to stand back and let them chart their own course.

When learners know that the learning belongs to them, that they aren't just a passive pair of ears, they will wake up, pay attention, and bring their own spirit and passion to the learning. They will be willing to take risks, make mistakes, challenge old beliefs, think for themselves, make decisions, act, create, and give the act of learning their total attention and their personal best.

Dave Meier sums it up with these inspirational thoughts:

The future belongs to the learners . . .
The learning that brings the brightest future
is learning that concentrates on . . .
how to work and live in a way that honors our humanity,
ignites the full range of all our intelligences,
and respects, nurtures, and preserves the earth.

—David Meier, *The Accelerated Learning*
Handbook (2000, p. 245)

Wrapping It Up

What a paradigm shift! From instructor-centered training to learner-centered training. From old, sit-down-and-listen instructional methods to new, stand-up-and-talk learning strategies. From monologue lectures to dialogue learning. From learning is delivery to learning is creation. A profound shift in perception!

The ideas and activities in this book are yours to experiment with, learn from, train with, and teach to others. They are meant to help you become better at what you do, fine-tune what you already do well, and create new ways of teaching and training that are even more successful for both you and your learners. Above all, this book is meant to inspire and celebrate you, your learners, and those you share it with.

Happy teaching and training! Here's a toast to you, the Ten-Minute Trainer!

Some changes are for good.
And this I know for sure:
Some things in life are meant to be,
Some changes set you free.

—Dionne Warwick

Early to Finish

Celebration. Stand up, raise your hands and arms in the air, and shout, "YES!" at the top of your lungs. Give yourself a high-ten! Shake hands or give hugs to anyone around—your family, friends, colleagues, coworkers, pets, plants, or stuffed animals.

Now go out and do something really nice for yourself to reaffirm the awesome work you do in educating others.

You DO make a difference. Know that. Celebrate that. And carry on!

Remarkable Resources

A Note from the Author

Here are some of my favorite resources, which will add to your knowledge of the concepts in *The Ten-Minute Trainer*. I've included personal comments for most of them. Rather than listing all the books in my training library, I've chosen the ones that I've used the most for my work.

These resources are divided into three sections, corresponding to the three numbered parts of *The Ten-Minute Trainer*. Some books could easily belong in all sections, even though I've listed them in just one. Use your own judgment when it comes to what you will find interesting and useful.

The wonderful thing about resources is that there is something for everyone. Not only do we like different types of books, Web sites, and the like, but each of us approaches reading material with different goals in mind. Ultimately, we learn different things from the same pages.

A cheer for us who revel in the research!

Part One

Bowman, Sharon. (2001). *Preventing death by lecture! Terrific tips for turning listeners into learners.* Glenbrook, NV: Bowperson Publishing. A short, easy read with dozens of quick activities—from one to five minutes in length—that a teacher or trainer can use with any subject and any size group. A must for making any lecture interactive and unforgettable.

Bowman, Sharon. (1999). *Shake, rattle, and roll! Using the ordinary to make your training extraordinary.* Glenbrook, NV: Bowperson Publishing. Over one hundred ways to use simple, ordinary objects and materials to create extraordinary learning experiences. Also includes many ways to use movement, music, and metaphor to make your message memorable.

Bowman, Sharon. (1997). *Presenting with pizzazz! Terrific tips for topnotch trainers.* Glenbrook, NV: Bowperson Publishing. A host of easy-to-apply tips and activities for getting learners of all ages more actively involved in their own learning.

Hoff, Ron. (1996). *Say it in six: How to say exactly what you mean in six minutes or less.* Kansas City, MO: Andrews and McMeel. For the time-conscious reader who wants to clarify and sharpen his or her speaking skills, presentations, or lectures. Includes practical ideas for presenting information in less time and with better results.

269

Silberman, Mel. (1995). *101 ways to make training active*. San Francisco: Jossey-Bass/Pfeiffer. One of the most extensive collections of active-learning techniques ever published. All of Mel's books are practical additions to a trainer's bookshelf.

Sugar, Steve. (1998). *Games that teach: Experiential activities for reinforcing training*. San Francisco: Jossey-Bass/Pfeiffer. A practical resource for trainers who have the time and desire to use fun, competitive games as review activities. All of Steve's books are useful additions to a trainer's bookshelf.

Thiagarajan, Sivasailam. (2003). *Design your own games and activities: Thiagi's templates for performance improvement*. San Francisco: Jossey-Bass/Pfeiffer. A comprehensive collection of Thiagi's best framegames, which are activities that a trainer can use with any training topic. Also includes the research and rationale behind using framegames as an integral part of training.

Part Two

Bowman, Sharon. (1998). *How to give it so they get it! A flight plan for teaching anyone anything and making it stick*. Glenbrook, NV: Bowperson Publishing. For readers who want to explore the ways they learn, teach, train, and communicate. Includes detailed descriptions of the four major learning styles and easy-to-follow instructions for forty experiential training activities. Also contains comprehensive chapters on the four-step Learning Styles Map, the forerunner to the Training Map in *The Ten-Minute Trainer*.

Hannaford, Carla. (1995). *Smart moves: Why learning is not all in your head*. Arlington, VA: Great Ocean Publishers. A compelling argument for the need to include the body in learning and the link between kinesthetic intelligence and long-term memory.

Hart, Leslie. (1983). *Human brain and human learning*. White Plains, NY: Longman. The granddaddy of all brain books. For readers who want to truly understand how the brain learns, and the disconnect between traditional, "school" learning and real learning. Includes a detailed chapter on the triune brain.

Howard, Pierce. (2000). *The owner's manual for the human brain: Everyday applications from mind-brain research*. Marietta, GA: Bard Press. Information packed and research based, this book is the "everything you wanted to know about the brain but were afraid to ask" resource for readers fascinated with how the human brain functions. Includes information about the reticular activating system and the triune brain.

Kolb, David. (1984). *Experiential learning: Experience as the source of learning and development*. Upper Saddle River, NJ: Prentice Hall. An esoteric view (and a very academic read) of how humans learn. The definitive research on "the natural cycle of learning," which is the basis for Learning the Natural Way in *The Ten-Minute Trainer*.

McCarthy, Bernice. (1996). *About learning*. Barrington, IL: Excel, Inc. A lyrical, "right-brain" approach to learning styles and the natural cycle of learning. It is also a detailed introduction to the 4MAT System of Instruction, which has its roots in David Kolb's research. Especially for classroom teachers.

Meier, David. (2000). *The accelerated learning handbook*. New York: McGraw-Hill. The most comprehensive book ever written about Accelerated Learning. Imminently practical, immediately useful, and filled with hundreds of ways to apply accelerated learning concepts. Includes Dave's Four Phases of Learning model, which is the foundation for the Training Map in *The Ten-Minute Trainer*. Also includes a multitude of great training strategies that are based on how people *really* learn, not on how they were conditioned to learn. A must for any teacher or trainer.

Meier, David. (1998). *The accelerated learning coursebuilder*. Lake Geneva, WI: Center for Accelerated Learning. A handsomely-boxed kit of six, spiral-bound books that cover all aspects of Accelerated Learning. Includes hundreds of activities that correspond to Dave's Four-Phase Learning Cycle. Also contains dozens of already-made course design models for popular training topics. Call 262-248-7070 for ordering information.

Palmer, Parker. (1998). *The courage to teach: Exploring the inner landscape of a teacher's life*. San Francisco: Jossey-Bass/Pfeiffer. A powerful and passionate testament to the importance of connections and community in teaching and learning. Explores the need for authentic community in classrooms in order to reclaim the true spirit of education. One quote says it all: "We teach who we are."

Rose, Colin, and Nicholl, Malcolm. (1997). *Accelerated learning for the 21st century*. New York: Dell. Another detailed look at Accelerated Learning and how to orchestrate instruction for maximum learning and retention. Includes a variety of ways to make training more effective.

Samples, Bob. (1987). *OpenMind/WholeMind: Parenting and teaching tomorrow's children today*. Rolling Hills Estates, CA: Jalmar Press. A very holistic and unique explanation of the human brain. Views the brain/mind as an "open" system and introduces the "holonomic" model of teaching and learning, that is, the connection and integration of parts to the whole of anything.

Sprenger, Marilee. (1999). *Learning and memory: The brain in action*. Alexandria, VA: Association for Supervision and Curriculum Development (ASCD). Excellent resource for understanding how memory works. Includes practical information about long-term memory and the roles that the triune brain and the reticular activating system play in memory storage and retrieval.

Stolovich, Harold. (2002). *Telling ain't training*. Alexandria, VA: American Society for Training & Development (ASTD). A highly engaging, "interactive" book that teaches through hands-on examples. Covers how humans learn and discusses how to meet those learning needs in training. Thought provoking, humorous, and immediately useful.

Sylwester, Robert. (1995). *A celebration of neurons: An educator's guide to the human brain.* Alexandria, VA: Association for Supervision and Curriculum Development (ASCD). The educational applications of new developments in brain and stress theory and research. Includes an excellent chapter on the importance of emotion and attention in learning, and information about the reticular activating system (reticular formation, as it's called in his book).

Part Three

Bach, Richard. (1977). *Illusions: The adventures of a reluctant messiah.* New York: Dell. Although this little book is more philosophical than educational, it does contain some quotable gems about how we learn, the best being, "We master what we teach."

Bromley, Karen, Irwin-De Vitis, Linda, and Modlo, Marcia. (1995). *Graphic organizers: Visual strategies for active learning.* New York: Scholastic Professional Books. Contains a variety of visual and spatial ways for learners to take notes and organize information.

Cambell, William, and Smith, Karl. (1997). *New paradigms for college teaching.* Minneapolis: Interaction Book Company. Although written with the college instructor in mind, this collection of thoughtful essays is valuable for anyone who teaches adults. Many of the essays' authors are notable educators who are working to change how adult education is delivered.

Charles, C. Leslie, and Clarke-Epstein, Chris. (1998). *The instant trainer: Quick tips on how to teach others what you know.* New York: McGraw-Hill. A delightful "Dear Abby" approach to learning about training, with two dedicated authors answering, in their own unique styles, common questions that trainers and would-be trainers ask. Includes a great appendix of immediately useful training tools.

DePorter, Bobbi. (1992). *Quantum learning: Unleashing the genius in you.* New York: Dell. A reader-friendly, hands-on learner's guide to learning and remembering.

El-Shamy, Susan. (2004). *How to design and deliver training for the new and emerging generations.* San Francisco: Pfeiffer. Covers both research and practical applications for teaching the generations following the Baby Boomer generation. Contains a wealth of easy ways to reach younger learners.

Gesell, Izzy. (1997). *Playing along: 37 group activities borrowed from improvisational theatre.* Duluth, MN: Whole Person Associates. A beginner's guide to using improvisation as a tool to spark creativity and active participation in the creative process.

Hunter, Madeline. (2003). *Enhancing teaching.* Upper Saddle River, NJ: Prentice-Hall. Written by one of the most influential voices in education in the United States, this resource compiles a century of educational and related research into practical classroom applications. Geared to the school educator.

Johnson, Spencer. (1986). *The one-minute teacher: How to teach others to teach themselves.* New York: William Morrow. A philosophical look at teaching and learning, with an emphasis on changing behavior.

Lowe, Robert. (2000). *Improvisation, Inc.—Harnessing spontaneity to engage people and groups.* San Francisco: Jossey-Bass/Pfeiffer. How to use the many creative benefits of improvisation to teach, train, and communicate.

Millbower, Lenn. (2000). *Training with a beat: The teaching power of music.* Sterling, VA: Stylus. An exploration of musical intelligence and the uses of music in learning.

Pike, Robert W. (2003). *Creative training techniques handbook: Tips, tactics, and how-to's for delivering effective training,* 3rd ed. Minneapolis: Lakewood Books. A detailed text that covers practical information about both training design and delivery. A trainer's basic how-to book.

Slan, Joanna. (1998). *Using stories and humor—Grab your audience!* Needham Heights, MA: Allyn and Bacon. A practical, down-to-earth guide for using stories as powerful speaking and training tools. Contains dozens of tips to help readers create their own original stories.

Slan, Joanna. (2001). *One-minute journaling.* St. Louis: EFG Publishing. Although the focus of this workbook is "Scrapbook Storytelling," it also provides a variety of quick journaling ideas for teachers and trainers. Delightfully illustrated and filled with quick writing tips. Enjoy Joanna's humorous comments about using journals, scrapbooks, and the writing process as memory tools.

St. Germain, Cliff. (2000). *Study whiz: A guide to better grades.* Chicago: Pivot Point International. An excellent resource for learners of all ages who wish to be successful in attaining their learning goals. Provides another way of looking at graphic organizers (the author calls them "Mind-Frames") and using these powerful visual-spatial tools to study and remember important information. Call 888-455-3276 for ordering information.

Thompson, Carolyn. (2000). *Creating highly interactive training quickly & effectively.* Frankfort, IL: Training Systems, Inc. A practical, step-by-step approach to designing training. Includes useful checklists for determining training needs and returns on investment. Call 800-469-3560 for ordering information.

Wacker, Mary B., and Silverman, Lori L. (2003). *Stories trainers tell: 55 ready-to-use stories to make training stick.* San Francisco: Jossey-Bass/Pfeiffer. Gives the reader useful tools for crafting memorable stories. Includes fifty-five ready-made stories that cover a variety of general training concepts and that readers have permission to use in their own training.

Westcott, Jean, and Hammond, Landau. (1997). *A picture's worth 1,000 words: A workbook for visual communications.* San Francisco: Jossey-Bass/Pfeiffer. Teaches the reader how to add simple yet powerful graphic images and pictures to any written information (charts, slides, handouts, and so forth). An easy, how-to resource to get the reader started.

Williams, Linda. (1983). *Teaching for the two-sided mind: A guide to right brain/left brain education.* New York: Simon & Schuster. Written for the classroom teacher but useful for corporate trainers also, this book has an excellent chapter on using metaphor as an instructional strategy. Also a good resource for understanding the two hemispheres of the cerebrum, or "thinking brain."

Extra Resources

Catalogs

The Brain Store (800-325-4769). Products and services on teaching, learning, and brain research. Also includes some unusual brain-related items.

Creative Training Techniques (800-383-9210). A great assortment of training books and learning aids. Especially for the busy trainer who wants some shortcuts in preparation time.

The Humor Project (800-225-0330). Upbeat items and books to help trainers add fun to their presentations.

Jossey-Bass/Pfeiffer (800-274-4434). An extensive variety of books, tapes, and other useful training resources.

Kipp Brothers (800-428-1153). A huge assortment of wholesale toys for bulk purchasing.

Lakeshore Learning Materials (800-421-5354). Supplier of children's educational toys, including "Model Magic," a unique white sculpting substance on which training participants can write.

Oriental Trading Company (800-228-2269). Unusual toy and craft items that can be bought in bulk.

The Trainer's Warehouse (800-299-3770). A fun and eclectic collection of products especially selected and developed to make training more hands-on and learner centered.

Web Sites

Note: These Web sites offer dozens of free downloadable tips, articles, and practical information for trainers and teachers. Some also offer free newsletters. All list products and services as well.

www.alcenter.com	The Center for Accelerated Learning David Meier, Director
www.activetraining.com	Active Training Mel Silberman, President
www.bobpikegroup.com	Creative Training Techniques, International Bob Pike, President
www.Bowperson.com	Bowperson Publishing and Training Sharon Bowman, Director
www.co-operation.org	The Cooperative Learning Center David and Roger Johnson, Directors
www.guilamuir.com	Guila Muir and Associates Guila Muir, President
www.thebrainstore.com	The Brain Store Eric Jensen, President
www.thiagi.com	The Thiagi Group Sivalsailam Thiagarajan, President and Mad Scientist
www.trainingsys.com	Training Systems, Inc. Carolyn Thompson, President

Many Thanks!

The following generous, creative people contributed specific ideas and activities to this book:

- Dave Meier, director of the Center for Accelerated Learning in Wisconsin, and my long-time friend and training mentor, who wrote the Foreword and who allowed me to freely quote him throughout the book.

- Peggy Reich, training director for Xanterra/Yellowstone National Park Lodges in Montana and Wyoming, who created the compass metaphor for her leadership training and then allowed me to borrow the metaphor for the Learning Compass.

- Tamara Chomenko-Cicero, lead technical trainer for Davis Wright Tremaine, who coined the phrase "Power-Hour" and generously allowed me to use it in creating the Power-Hour Training Templates.

- Diane Cheatwood, member of the Board of Directors for Teaching for a Change in Colorado, who created the fabulous Walkabout activity and gladly offered it to me to include in the book.

- DeeAnn Woitena, principal of Jackson Intermediate School of the Pasadena Independent School District in Texas, who shared the Quick Start idea with me.

- Jeani McGrath, fellow educator, speaker, and director of Journeys with Jeani, who created the energetic Pop-Up activity format and graciously agreed to its inclusion in the book.

- The Web site www.clipart.com, the extensive source of original graphics from which this book's final graphics were created.

The following kind and patient people helped with the book production and editing:

- Martin Delahoussaye, Pfeiffer's senior editor, who had enough faith in me to say that he wouldn't let this book get away, and who was forever kind and encouraging.

- Steve Sugar, my training colleague, who helped polish the manuscript with his own creative hints.

- Kathleen Dolan Davies, Pfeiffer's director of development, who patiently waited for the manuscript through the time of my mother's passing.
- Nina Kreiden, Pfeiffer's production editor, who kept me advised of the production process with newsy, cheerful e-notes.
- Janis Chan, Pfeiffer's developmental editor, and Suzanne Copenhagen, Pfeiffer's copyeditor, who both went through the manuscript with a fine-tooth comb and provided excellent editing expertise and positive feedback.
- Mary Gillot, Pfeiffer's illustrator, who brought the book's graphics to life.
- Arthur VanGundy, who also offered his editing labors and who enthusiastically praised the book's concepts.
- Diane Turso, who polished the page proofs with her excellent editing skills.

The following family and friends gave time, support, and love, especially when I needed it the most:

- Ross Barnett, my partner for life, who listened, cared, cheered me on, served me late-night cups of tea, and was there whenever I needed him.
- My aunt, Margaret Cote, who stayed by my side through Mom's passing, and who fed me afterwards while I wrote.
- Don and Marie Bowman, my brother and sister-in-law, who checked in regularly and saw to it that I got a break now and then.
- My cousins Raenele Cote and Michele Shomaker, who supported me and let me cry when I needed to.
- Jan Thurman, my best friend, who reframed Mom's passing for me so that I could grieve, heal, and write.
- The Barnetts—Meredith, Jeremy, Lucille, and Ken—who called, wrote, and offered their own words of condolences and encouragement.
- My mastermind friends—Marcia Jackson, Carol Kivler, and Marianne Frederick—and my training buddy Laura Moriarty, who sent me loving e-mails, made encouraging calls, and let me know how much they cared.
- My dear Indiana family, Joyce Duvall and Gene Critchfield, whose supportive e-mails and loving advice also helped me through the difficult times.

- Barbie Hoefer, Val Engebretson, Charlene Meenan, Mary Ann Boyd, Andy Deane, Maureen Missett, Martha Dow, Teresa Schroeder, and all my Glenbrook neighbors, who asked me for progress reports and shouted "Hurray!" when the book was done.

- All my family members and friends, close and far, whose kind words, e-mails, calls, and conversations meant more to me than they will ever know.

- And, of course, Frances Bowman, my mom, who, when she was alive, encouraged and advised and loved me—and certainly is doing it still.

To all, thank you from the bottom of my heart—and top—and all parts in between!

Sharon L. Bowman
Glenbrook at Lake Tahoe, Nevada

About the Author

Meet Sharon L. Bowman:

- Professional speaker and corporate trainer
- Staff development consultant and instructor for school districts and colleges
- Author of seven popular training and motivation books
- Director, The Lake Tahoe Trainers Group
- Professional Member, National Speakers Association

Sharon Bowman shows trainers how to "teach it quick and make it stick." She also shows learners how to "learn it fast and make it last." She works with people who want to fine-tune their information-giving skills, and businesses that want to offer exceptional in-house training programs.

Sharon turns passive listeners into active learners with her high-energy, hands-on approach to presenting and training. Her classes and seminars are practical, useful, memorable, and fun. Over 60,000 of her first six popular training and motivation books are now in print.

Sharon delivers interactive keynotes and conference sessions, and customized, public, and in-house training programs. She is also the trainer's coach, helping individual teachers and trainers polish existing courses and create new programs that reach all learners.

For more information about Sharon Bowman and her books and training services, log onto www.Bowperson.com, or e-mail her at Sharon@Bowperson.com or SBowperson@aol.com.

Pfeiffer Publications Guide

This guide is designed to familiarize you with the various types of Pfeiffer publications. The formats section describes the various types of products that we publish; the methodologies section describes the many different ways that content might be provided within a product. We also provide a list of the topic areas in which we publish.

FORMATS

In addition to its extensive book-publishing program, Pfeiffer offers content in an array of formats, from fieldbooks for the practitioner to complete, ready-to-use training packages that support group learning.

FIELDBOOK Designed to provide information and guidance to practitioners in the midst of action. Most fieldbooks are companions to another, sometimes earlier, work, from which its ideas are derived; the fieldbook makes practical what was theoretical in the original text. Fieldbooks can certainly be read from cover to cover. More likely, though, you'll find yourself bouncing around following a particular theme, or dipping in as the mood, and the situation, dictate.

HANDBOOK A contributed volume of work on a single topic, comprising an eclectic mix of ideas, case studies, and best practices sourced by practitioners and experts in the field.

An editor or team of editors usually is appointed to seek out contributors and to evaluate content for relevance to the topic. Think of a handbook not as a ready-to-eat meal, but as a cookbook of ingredients that enables you to create the most fitting experience for the occasion.

RESOURCE Materials designed to support group learning. They come in many forms: a complete, ready-to-use exercise (such as a game); a comprehensive resource on one topic (such as conflict management) containing a variety of methods and approaches; or a collection of like-minded activities (such as icebreakers) on multiple subjects and situations.

TRAINING PACKAGE An entire, ready-to-use learning program that focuses on a particular topic or skill. All packages comprise a guide for the facilitator/trainer and a workbook for the participants. Some packages are supported with additional media—such as video—or learning aids, instruments, or other devices to help participants understand concepts or practice and develop skills.

- *Facilitator/trainer's guide* Contains an introduction to the program, advice on how to organize and facilitate the learning event, and step-by-step instructor notes. The guide also contains copies of presentation materials—handouts, presentations, and overhead designs, for example—used in the program.

- *Participant's workbook* Contains exercises and reading materials that support the learning goal and serves as a valuable reference and support guide for participants in the weeks and months that follow the learning event. Typically, each participant will require his or her own workbook.

ELECTRONIC CD-ROMs and web-based products transform static Pfeiffer content into dynamic, interactive experiences. Designed to take advantage of the searchability, automation, and ease-of-use that technology provides, our e-products bring convenience and immediate accessibility to your workspace.

METHODOLOGIES

CASE STUDY A presentation, in narrative form, of an actual event that has occurred inside an organization. Case studies are not prescriptive, nor are they used to prove a point; they are designed to develop critical analysis and decision-making skills. A case study has a specific time frame, specifies a sequence of events, is narrative in structure, and contains a plot structure—an issue (what should be/have been done?). Use case studies when the goal is to enable participants to apply previously learned theories to the circumstances in the case, decide what is pertinent, identify the real issues, decide what should have been done, and develop a plan of action.

ENERGIZER A short activity that develops readiness for the next session or learning event. Energizers are most commonly used after a break or lunch to stimulate or refocus the group. Many involve some form of physical activity, so they are a useful way to counter post-lunch lethargy. Other uses include transitioning from one topic to another, where "mental" distancing is important.

EXPERIENTIAL LEARNING ACTIVITY (ELA) A facilitator-led intervention that moves participants through the learning cycle from experience to application (also known as a Structured Experience). ELAs are carefully thought-out designs in which there is a definite learning purpose and intended outcome. Each step—everything that participants do during the activity—facilitates the accomplishment of the stated goal. Each ELA includes complete instructions for facilitating the intervention and a clear statement of goals, suggested group size and timing, materials required, an explanation of the process, and, where appropriate, possible variations to the activity. (For more detail on Experiential Learning Activities, see the Introduction to the *Reference Guide to Handbooks and Annuals*, 1999 edition, Pfeiffer, San Francisco.)

GAME A group activity that has the purpose of fostering team spirit and togetherness in addition to the achievement of a pre-stated goal. Usually contrived—undertaking a desert expedition, for example—this type of learning method offers an engaging means for participants to demonstrate and practice business and interpersonal skills. Games are effective for team building and personal development mainly because the goal is subordinate to the process—the means through which participants reach decisions, collaborate, communicate, and generate trust and understanding. Games often engage teams in "friendly" competition.

ICEBREAKER A (usually) short activity designed to help participants overcome initial anxiety in a training session and/or to acquaint the participants with one another. An icebreaker can be a fun activity or can be tied to specific topics or training goals. While a useful tool in itself, the icebreaker comes into its own in situations where tension or resistance exists within a group.

INSTRUMENT A device used to assess, appraise, evaluate, describe, classify, and summarize various aspects of human behavior. The term used to describe an instrument depends primarily on its format and purpose. These terms include survey, questionnaire, inventory, diagnostic, survey, and poll. Some uses of instruments include providing instrumental feedback to group members, studying here-and-now processes or functioning within a group, manipulating group composition, and evaluating outcomes of training and other interventions.

Instruments are popular in the training and HR field because, in general, more growth can occur if an individual is provided with a method for focusing specifically on his or her own behavior. Instruments also are used to obtain information that will serve as a basis for change and to assist in workforce planning efforts.

Paper-and-pencil tests still dominate the instrument landscape with a typical package comprising a facilitator's guide, which offers advice on administering the instrument and interpreting the collected data, and an initial set of instruments. Additional instruments are available separately. Pfeiffer, though, is investing heavily in e-instruments. Electronic instrumentation provides effortless distribution and, for larger groups particularly, offers advantages over paper-and-pencil tests in the time it takes to analyze data and provide feedback.

LECTURETTE A short talk that provides an explanation of a principle, model, or process that is pertinent to the participants' current learning needs. A lecturette is intended to establish a common language bond between the trainer and the participants by providing a mutual frame of reference. Use a lecturette as an introduction to a group activity or event, as an interjection during an event, or as a handout.

MODEL A graphic depiction of a system or process and the relationship among its elements. Models provide a frame of reference and something more tangible, and more easily remembered, than a verbal explanation. They also give participants something to "go on," enabling them to track their own progress as they experience the dynamics, processes, and relationships being depicted in the model.

ROLE PLAY A technique in which people assume a role in a situation/scenario: a customer service rep in an angry-customer exchange, for example. The way in which the role is approached is then discussed and feedback is offered. The role play is often repeated using a different approach and/or incorporating changes made based on feedback received. In other words, role playing is a spontaneous interaction involving realistic behavior under artificial (and safe) conditions.

SIMULATION A methodology for understanding the interrelationships among components of a system or process. Simulations differ from games in that they test or use a model that depicts or mirrors some aspect of reality in form, if not necessarily in content. Learning occurs by studying the effects of change on one or more factors of the model. Simulations are commonly used to test hypotheses about what happens in a system—often referred to as "what if?" analysis—or to examine best-case/worst-case scenarios.

THEORY A presentation of an idea from a conjectural perspective. Theories are useful because they encourage us to examine behavior and phenomena through a different lens.

TOPICS

The twin goals of providing effective and practical solutions for workforce training and organization development and meeting the educational needs of training and human resource professionals shape Pfeiffer's publishing program. Core topics include the following:

Leadership & Management

Communication & Presentation

Coaching & Mentoring

Training & Development

E-Learning

Teams & Collaboration

OD & Strategic Planning

Human Resources

Consulting